Candice Bloch

About the Author

Michael Tunison is a sports blogger and freelance writer. The coeditor of the NFL blog Kissing Suzy Kolber, Tunison is also a contributing writer for Dead-spin, With Leather, Pro Football Talk, and Yahoo's Shut-down Corner. He lives in Alexandria, Virginia.

THE FOOTBALL FAN'S MANIFESTO

THE FOOTBALL FAN'S MANIFESTO

MICHAEL TUNISON

itbooks

An Imprint of **HarperCollins**Publishers

*it***books**

HarperCollins books may be purchased for educational, business, or
sales promotional use. For information please write: Special Markets
Department, HarperCollins Publishers, 10 East 53rd Street, New York,
NY 10022.

FIRST EDITION

Illustrated by Rob Ullman
Designed by Renato Stanisic

Library of Congress Cataloging-in-Publication Data
Tunison, Michael.
The football fan's manifesto / Michael Tunison.
p. cm.
ISBN 978-0-06-173514-1
1. Football—Miscellanea. I. Title.
GV951.T86 2009
796.332—dc22   2009007035

09 10 11 12 13   OV/RRD   10 9 8 7 6 5 4 3 2 1

*To my mother, with all my love,
even if she is a Redskins fan*

CONTENTS

ARTICLE IX: TAKE FANDOM TO UNHEALTHY LEVELS—THEN A LITTLE FURTHER 247

ARTICLE X: DEATH: BECAUSE ONLY AL DAVIS CAN LIVE FOREVER 287

ACKNOWLEDGMENTS

This book would not exist without the work of Johan Gutenberg, Al Gore, and the Rooney family. Also, these people:

First and foremost, my family: my mom and dad, Christina, Angie, Marissa, Alexandra, and Colleen.

My second, hipper, blacker family: Kevin Merida and Donna Britt, who drove me to start writing and are therefore responsible for every bad joke in this book; the immensely talented Hamani Britt-Gibson, who owes me twenty dollars; and my weekly football confidant and TV murderer Darrell Britt-Gibson.

Internet dick-joke-slinging brethren: Drew Magary, Matt Ufford, Jack Kogod, Joshua Zerkle, and the shadowy figure that is flubby. As well as our Uproxx benefactors Jarret Myer and Brian Brater. And Jerry Thompson, who makes it run smoothly.

JoAnn Bruch, to whom I owe my all-consuming football fanaticism.

My editor Matthew Benjamin: You took a chance on me and made this mystifying process remarkably easy. Apologies again for all the bukkake jokes in the first draft.

Much thanks to my compatriots in Web-based onanistic sportswriting for continued support, inspiration, and Brazzers.com log-ins: Will Leitch, Nick Dallamora, Sarah Sprague, Mike Florio, Stefan Fatsis, DJ Gallo, Spencer Hall, Brian Powell, Raquel Frisardi, Dan Shanoff, Matt Johnson, Gourmet Spud, Brooks Melchior, The Mighty MJD, Vince Mancini, Dan Levy, Chris Cooley, Wright Thompson, Cajun Boy, Chris Cotter, Michael Grass, Rob Iracane, J. E. Skeets, Grimey, Scott Van Pelt, the Brothers Mottram, Sarah Schorno, Dan Steinberg, Enrico Campitelli Jr., and A. J. Daulerio.

Friends, well-wishers, and people who don't wish me any specific harm: Ralston Yorrick, Jessica Rinne, Aaron Andzik, Joe Nese, Barbara Lindell, Vanessa Parra, Lana Chung, Rob Ullman, Candice Bloch, Jon Lewis, Elahe Izadi, Ben Domenech, Adam Claus, and Rachel Freedenberg.

Katie, Sterling, Nena, Sal, Scrappy, Jobie, and the rest of folks at the Pour House with whom I share my boozy autumn Sundays and screaming fits.

The readers and commenters at Kissing Suzy Kolber: When they aren't cussing me out or dismissively commenting "meh" on my posts, they're making me eternally grateful not to be writing any more ten-inch stories on county council meetings. Thanks, assholes!

THE
FOOTBALL
FAN'S
MANIFESTO

ARTICLE I

The Supremacy of Football

I.1 Other Major Sports Are Inherently Inferior to Pro Football and Therefore Unworthy of Our Time.

Professional football is the undisputed god-king of American sports. It always has been so, even back in the times when we hadn't quite realized it yet. The mere existence of pro football obviates the need for all other contests of athletic skill, yet these other "sports" (parlor games, really) remain despite their complete and utter irrelevance. Why we abide by such unnecessary, quasi-athletic diversions when we have the game of football is a testament to our modern excess.

To be fair, these other "sports" do serve some minor purpose. And not only to give us something to mock. Because the NFL has yet to genetically produce elite athletes able to withstand the rigors of a year-round schedule (why the hold up?), we're left with nearly seven desolate months of no meaningful football. During these dark times of despair, some of these lesser sports are all we have to stave off the clammy hands of adult responsibilities and a social life. They're passable, if barely adequate, distractions to fill the hours until the late summer rolls around. That's all. Nothing more. Certainly nothing to get worked up about.

However—and it should come as a great shock—there are depraved individuals out there who maintain that some of these other "sports" can produce a level of enjoyment on par with the NFL. The sickest among these deviants even insist that others sports can provide a *preferable* viewing experience to professional football. As if such a thing were actually possible. Wrongheaded as this belief is, our permissive, increasingly soccer-tolerant culture has allowed it to propagate in certain circles with an air of acceptance. It's high time we set the record straight. In doing so, hopefully we can reach these woefully misinformed souls before they do something unforgivable like purchase season tickets to the Red Sox.

Baseball—In 1987, *Washington Post* columnist Thomas Boswell memorably attempted, and epically failed, to enumerate ninety-nine reasons why baseball is better than football. Of course it didn't take him more than five to screw the whole thing up. Singing "Take Me Out to the Ball Game" at Wrigley Field is supposed to be a virtue? I guess that's a possibility if one were to disregard the famously awful renditions by Ozzy Osbourne, Jeff Gordon, and dozens of other celebrity duffers. More to the point, the Major League

Baseball regular season lasts approximately two and a half lifetimes and feels at least three times that long. A *Lord of the Rings* movie doesn't drag on as much. By the time it gets halfway interesting in September and October, football season has already begun. Poor timing on your part, *besuboru*. Half the players in the league now require the services of an interpreter to tell fans to fuck off (at least have the courtesy to cuss me out in my own language, Ichiro). The game falls back on its puffed-up long-gone era of cultural import; meanwhile, MLB *playoff* games draw about half the audience of an NFL regular season contest. And any sport that considers Bartolo Colon an athlete immediately gets bumped down to second-tier status. At least the fatties in football can block. Unless they play for the Rams.

Basketball—Thanks, but I prefer to stick with sports that I know are only *probably* fixed. Not to mention those whose leagues aren't teetering on the brink of insolvency. Contraction is a very real threat for several NBA teams, which figures to ruin the lives of nearly dozens of rabid hoop fans. Besides, the NBA Playoffs drag on about as long as the baseball regular season. The perennial powerhouse Spurs might be the most unlikeable team in all of sports. The most compelling story line in recent years is the never-ending drama surrounding LeBron James's eventual departure from Cleveland, as though anyone found LeBron even remotely likeable. And, okay, sure, college basketball is a hoot (for about a month, anyway), but anything that Duke excels at is ruined for all parties involved. Not to mention the disconcerting correlation between getting older and the creepiness of getting emotional about teenagers committing to a certain school.

College Football—The bastard cousin of professional football exists solely as a refuge for aged frat boys and Southerners. Proponents will harangue you endlessly about its superiority to the pro game, claiming that the atmosphere at a college football game is far more raucous than its professional counterpart and that student athletes play for love, not money (okay, love, under-the-table gifts from the university, the promise of future riches, boylike adulation from boosters, and poon up to your hairline). All this is actually fairly accurate, but ultimately moot, because the NCAA refuses to implement a playoff system, opting to continue with its convoluted Bowl Championship Series, which leads to the annual screwing of more deserving teams in favor of USC and Ohio State. It may be true that the way college football conducts overtime is technically fairer, since each team is guaranteed at least one possession. Problem is, it takes goddamn forever. I will say in college football's defense that at least Duke sucks at it.

Soccer—Soccer fans will never fail to remind you

that there are more people around the globe who follow "the Beautiful Game" than what they dismissively refer to as "American football." That's all well and good, Ronaldinminihinho, but there are also more people around the world living in abject poverty than in America, so let's all jump on that bandwagon too!

Rugby—I'm not even sure rugby fans actually like their sport so much as they enjoy snottily explaining to you how much tougher rugby is than football because rugby players don't wear helmets or pads. Rugby could actually be fun to watch, but you'll get so tired of the bombardment of smug coming from the guy who spent a summer abroad in Australia that you'll never actually bother to check it out. That, and their fans wear scarves. You know the other type of fans who love scarves? Harry Potterphiles. From this we can conclude that rugby is one step removed from Quidditch.

NASCAR—Fess up, racing fans. This is just an excuse to spend an entire day getting plastered, isn't it? Not that football isn't, but at least football fans don't make it quite so obvious. Nor do they need a hefty supply of OxyContin to make it through the sheer crushing repetition that is watching cars circle a track eight thousand times.

Formula One—Like NASCAR, but for foreigners, meaning it's even more boring and nobody is allowed to pass anyone else.

Tennis—If the argument in favor of tennis doesn't begin and end with Ana Ivanovic, Serena Williams, and Maria Sharapova, then you're wasting your breath. Your heaving, luscious breath. Whew. Excuse me.

Golf—Mark Twain's famed axiom that the game is "a good walk spoiled" doesn't quite tell the whole story. It's a waste of a lot of money too. Sure, Tiger Woods is amazing, but even when he plays injured, he still blows the field away. Where's the drama in that? John Daly does tailgate like a pro, however.

Boxing—Because the sweet science has been off the radar of the casual sports fan for such a long period of time, it's mostly the purists that have hung on to keep this sport afloat. And my God, they're fucking annoying.

Scripps National Spelling Bee—Most viewers would not categorize a spelling bee as a sporting contest, but there it is on ESPN each spring. Worse than watching the Indian kid get screwed out of the title every year is observing all the twee Decemberist-listening pseudo-intellectual fans fetishizing a contest that requires inflexible rote memorization and no imagination while crowing about how they can spell "postlapsarian" off the top of their head. I hope they get run over by a newspaper truck.

Bowling—Jerome Bettis once bowled a 300 game, which proves anyone can bowl their weight. It just so happens that this corresponds to a perfect game.

Billiards—Difficult to back a sport where ads for instructional tapes on how to make trick shots are more entertaining than the sport itself.

World Series of Poker—Two journalists have written captivating books about trying their hands at playing professional football. Though *Paper Lion* and *A Few Seconds of Panic* are thrilling accounts of the exploits of George Plimpton with the Detroit Lions and Stefan Fatsis with the Denver Broncos, it is clear they are overwhelmed by the level of competition that they face. Meanwhile, writer James Mc-Manus takes a crack at the World Series of Poker in *Positively Fifth Street* and damn near wins the whole tournament. Viz: If a journalist can do it well, it isn't a sport.

Hockey—I thought we were only covering major sports here. Okay, okay. Easy now, hockey fans. Don't go pelting my house with squid. I know your sport is enjoying a minor resurgence in recent years. That's gotta put you on pace to overtake the runaway freight train of popularity that is the rock paper scissors championship circuit any year now.

I.2 A People's History of Football Fanaticism

It was back in the time of the ancients (sometime pre-merger, I believe) that God gave unto man His only be-gotten sport, that of the most holy game of football. Man, being mired in benighted acts of civilization-building and fundamental scientific discovery, was not yet ready to accept this altogether amazing gift. Instead, humankind pissed away centuries occupying itself with the disgusting perversions of soccer and rugby before eventually coming to its collective senses. As with most things, the blame can be laid at the unwashed, hairy feet of the Europeans.

The figure responsible for humanity's overdue crawl from the muck was a man named Walter Camp, a visionary American hero in the truest and most badassed sense, despite the fact that he attended Yale and was therefore probably a privileged asshole. Camp saw the flaws inherent in lesser football imitations and implemented critical changes, including establishing the line of scrimmage, down-and-distance rules, and the two-point safety, and making what can be considered a holding penalty as vague and open to arbitrary interpretation by referees as possible. Soon, a golden age was born.

In the generations since Camp laid these foundations of the game, professional football has supplanted baseball as our country's most popular sport. Football accomplished this with the canny strategy of offering a spectacle that's actually interesting and fun to watch. Somehow that seemed to resonate with people. This was not always the case. Long ago, the leather-headed greats of the past lined up in austere formations and dove into sloppy, sepia-toned piles. It was kind of like how the Tennessee Titans run their offense nowadays, sans LenDale White shedding fast-food wrappers as he waddles down the field.

Much has changed in the NFL's roughly ninety years of operation. It's a much more offensively oriented game now. A defender who even so much as thinks of hitting an opposing quarterback or receiver outside his league-mandated "contact zone" (a two-inch area located on the chest between the jersey numbers) stands to get penalized for roughing the passer or pass interference and likely charged with second-degree aggravated assault (first degree if they have the gall to tackle him).

One thing that has not changed is the endlessly intricate and nacho-intensive nature of football fandom. Even with modern game-neutering provisions (if you can't horse-collar tackle, how is Roy Williams expected to play the game?), the visceral excitement of watching pro football is without equal. That is, unless you're a fan of the Detroit Lions, in which case crocheting oven cozies is probably as engrossing and certainly more rewarding. In its ascension to the lofty heights of utterly ineffable awesomeness, the game has come to be littered with a multitude of arcane procedures, involved formations, and labyrinthine rules. For most players, the learning curve is measured in years and drunk-driving arrests. Football fandom has no fewer complexities, filled as it is with an endless supply of argued-over details, unspoken rules, and Byzantine game-day routines. Lacking an ironclad catechism for fandom, tons of NFL followers succumb to the pitfalls of face-painting, pink jerseys, and network pregame shows each year. This is a sad fate to befall anyone, even the already unfortunate fans in Green Bay.

To be a truly hard-core fan, one must be inured to the highly regimented lifestyle that drives grown men to invest all of their emotional energy, lingering shreds of sanity, and disposable income to live vicariously through other, over-grown men they'll probably never meet (and if they do, wish they hadn't), who are paid handsomely by a corporation with yearly revenue in the billions. Other than their seven-figure salaries, extensive perks, and adulation, what do these athletes have to live for? Fans give these men purpose, and they in turn give fans a figure of worship. The circle of life, it twirls on. Will you, the fan, be asked to sacrifice to keep it moving? No, because asking implies that you have an option. Baseball fans ask. That's why they fail.

I.3 The Football Fan Is the Next Evolution of Man

To the layperson, the above football fan may come across as contented and entertained, if not in an alcohol-induced catatonic state. But behind the drunken haze lies a troubled and sorely bereft fan aching for the most basic accoutrements of true NFL fanhood. Where is his laptop to get live fantasy scoring updates? Is he watching on HD with a satellite package or simply relying on national networks to dictate which game he watches? His food options are also shockingly thin, to say nothing of the staggering lack of NFL licensed gear adorning his person. If his team is to perform well, who is he to mock? If they lose, who can he get into a fist fight with?

This man deserves better. Likely he is only carving out a meager allotment of time with football so that later he can repair to what he considers to be more important tasks. That's bullshit, of course. Fanhood is bigger than life. It's part of the larger cause of advancing the interests of your team. Football fans oftentimes get a bad rap. We are considered the most boorish, the most idiotic, the most violent, and the most Zubaz-pants clad of all spectators in the sporting world. All this, of course, is completely true, but is that such a bad thing? Well, except the Zubaz pants—those things really are horrendous. The rest you should embrace.

Counting sixteen regular season games, up to four postseason games (fans of the Bengals, Rams, Lions, and Raiders please disregard), four or five agonizingly pointless preseason games, the Pro Bowl, and the two days of the draft, fans get less than one full month each year to spend watching their favorite team do anything remotely football-related. The other 330 or so days are about filling blank space, a task that becomes more and more difficult with each passing off-season. Seriously, any chance we can get some free tickets for having to go through that shit? At least a team schedule printed on a refrigerator magnet? Anything?

To make matters worse, with each year football as we knew and loved it is being wrest away. Roger "Fidel" Goodell, in his brief tenure as commissioner, has shown the unyielding iron fist of a tyrant in trying to shape the league into the anodyne version of football that he has convinced himself will broaden its appeal. Included in his authoritarian bag of tricks are expanding and cracking down on what he considers an excessive show of force on the field with an outrageously liberal application of fines. At the same time, Goodell autocratically attempts to curb our American-born right to enjoy football as loutishly as we like with an oppressive fan-conduct policy. In response to a spate of fines of his teammates, Troy Polamalu (the heavily tressed Pro Bowl safety of the Pittsburgh Steelers), dubbed the machinations of exalted chairman Goodell as the transformation of the NFL into a "pansy league." Though Polamalu was only referring to the tactics Goodell has employed to neuter the sport of its core toughness on the field, we would like to think the soft-spoken but hard-hitting Samoan was also alluding to the lengths the Ginger Generalissimo has gone to Disney-fy the game on its periphery, alienating its established base of fans in favor of attracting the kind of lifeless, halfhearted spectators who characterize a baseball crowd.

The metaphor of football as warfare has always struck some as ridiculous, but in recent years it has become more apt, if only for the way armed conflicts and professional football are presented to us in increasingly sanitized ways. Certainly, the ugliness is scrubbed from each for different reasons: war, so the country can continue to wage them without losing public opinion; football, so the league can cozy up to tight-assed corporations and the so-called family market those companies covet. But we want the truth, warts and all. The game is dirty, violent, and ugly and meant both to excite us and make us a bit uncomfortable. In turn, we should not be expected to act like we're watching a match at Wimbledon.

To those with the fortitude and the desire to meet the standards of a steel-willed, ravaged-livered fanatic, I urge you to press on, flask and giant foam finger in hand. Being a true fan is a lifelong commitment more demanding than either your career or your marriage (that is, if you happen to be saddled with such things—please note that they are fine distractions for the spring and summer but they only serve as encumbrances come autumn time). Ultimately, it's the fandom that sustains you and gives you purpose, not to mention a socially acceptable excuse to get sloppy drunk for weekends at a time. More importantly, it gives you a fellowship with others who follow the creed and live the code. These are the people who understand you, who spill beer on you and call you nasty hate-filled epithets in the parking lot. In short, they are extensions of yourself, but in a way that doesn't make you sexually uncomfortable. Well, most of the time. People can be excused for getting carried away when the team wins.

The Fundamentals of Fandom

II.1 Pick a Team, Any Team. Just Pick One and Only One

Picking a team is the most important decision of your life, so don't screw it up by picking the Lions and know what you're getting into if you pick the Cowboys (being loathed). Time is of the essence, so don't be like Brett Favre and drag out your decision for an eternity. The absolute deadline to pick a team is your eighth birthday. Before that, you are in sports infancy and can be as willy-nilly and band-wagon-prone with your fandom as your wee widdle heart desires. Up until the third grade, kids don't understand even the basic principles and pathologies of rooting for a team. Because kids are stupid. At that critical eighth year, something activates in the brain that solidifies sports allegiance. Ask any neurologist, they'll back me up on this. It's science. Political leanings can be fluid. You can have an epiphany later in life that can make you change parties, change philosophies, hell, even change gender, but if at any point after that eighth birthday, even so much as one day later you switch teams, you are rendered a failure as a person and subject to public shunning and completely justified brutality.

There are any number of factors that can determine who your favorite team may be. For most, it's a matter of where they spent their childhood or who their parents pulled for. These are perfectly reasonable and probably the most universally accepted justifications for liking a team. But they should not be considered the only ones.

Contrary to the hometown rule, you can latch onto a team for any number of superficial reasons. For example, Chiefs fans share a common love for suffering multiple heart attacks before the age of forty. Others may be captivated by one superstar athlete. You can be stuck in an area that skirts several fan-base boundaries. Hell, you can adopt a team for otherwise contemptible causes, picking one that wins all the time or even one that has uniforms and a logo you like. For the latter two, you're going to have to make up another excuse when someone asks you the origin of your fandom. Under no circumstances should you divulge those disgraceful enticements.

What matters most here is the timing. As long as you commit to a team early enough in life, no one can question you for it. Though they will find a way to insult you, it's because that's the way football discourse works. And, of course, you can never switch teams for any reason other than your team relocating from a city. If the overwhelming power of your allegiance demands you to follow that team to its new hometown, more power to you, but you are by no means compelled to do so. Just remember, don't pick the Browns. Or the Bills. And God help you if you end up with the Texans. But then, He only helps those who help themselves, leaving you doubly forsaken.

2.2 Who You Root for Defines Who You Are

Maybe you thought the choice of your favorite team really was an offhand decision you could make based solely on who has the coolest uniforms or which player endorsed your favorite car dealership. Maybe think again. Even though Haroldson's Toyota is the tits, there are many other more important considerations, life-lasting ones, to account for before making this most critical selection.

No matter which team you settle on as you own, a set of prevailing stereotypes and shorthand associations will immediately be assigned to you by fans of other teams and by the media at large. Knowing these beforehand will prove instructive and may inform your selection process. After all, you'll want to know why everybody else at Gillette Stadium only boos the black players.

Arizona Cardinals—Now that the team's been to a Super Bowl, people actually realize that you exist. Moreover, once the team made it to the dance, Arizona Cardinals fans themselves finally came into existence, as if the NFC championship victory over the Eagles were a big bang to begin the Arizonaverse.

Prior to that, any Cardinals-following was about as tangible as the campus of the University of Phoenix, the unfortunate naming rights holders for the team's stadium in Glendale.

Atlanta Falcons—Your threshold for dogfighting jokes is shorter than most, though you can't deny the appeal of the occasional canine brawl to the death. It's a cultural thing, after all. Pulling for the Falcons makes you an ardent Home Depot apologist and leaves you unable to watch a football game unless a Ludacris track is heard every stoppage in play. If you're white and dancing the Dirty Bird, you've waived any legal expectation not to be dragged from the back of a truck. Same goes for anyone who considers Matty Ice an acceptable name for a crappy domestic beer, let alone a quarterback.

Baltimore Ravens—Wait, what's that? What happened to your legs? I can't see them with those purple-tinged army camouflage pants you've got on. Those must come in handy when engaging in tactical military missions in fields of lilacs. Yes, Baltimore is the proud home of John Waters, and therefore a bastion of tackiness, but c'mon. Just because you can doesn't mean you should. I only mean to poke fun, Ravens fans. I'd hate for your defense to take out a bounty on me.

Buffalo Bills—Oh Lord. You poor wretched thing. The pain you've been through. The crushing disappointment, the wrenching stench of defeat, the unbearable suffering that comes with each passing day. Oh, I'm just talking about living in Buffalo. You root for the Bills too? Quite the glutton for punishment, aren't we? No wonder you signed Terrell Owens.

Carolina Panthers—The Panthers made it to the NFC Championship Game in only their second year of existence and had a Super Bowl appearance in their first decade, so fans have had it a little better than most during the team's brief run. (Still, they'd give it all up for one more national championship for the Tar Heels.) Don't envy them too much, though. They've each had a relative gunned down by Rae Carruth in callously indifferent blood.

Chicago Bears—A team with a hard-nosed tradition and a proud history is bound to foster some committed fans. But when those committed fans assume that every iota of team news, no matter how esoteric, is worthy of universal attention, that's when you must forcibly sterilize them with garden shears. To their credit, Bears fans, and players alike, can cultivate a damn fine neck beard.

Cincinnati Bengals—You've been conditioned to despise owner Mike Brown and continually live in despair, yet you still manage to root for the least embarrassing modern-era team in your state. Go you! Being a fan of the only Ohio team to reach a Super Bowl can be a heady experience. Try not to be too smug to the Browns fans when the Bengals pick up their third win

in Week 16. The team's brief flirtation with respect-
ability brought with it a reputation for lawlessness.
Fortunately, the Bengals have cleaned up their act and,
in doing so, have plunged back into irrelevancy. No
wonder they keep bringing back Chris Henry.

Cleveland Browns—The milkbone in your mouth
lost its flavor months ago. Your sons are named for
Bernie Kosar and your daughters for Brady Quinn.
Lawlessness is certain to descend upon the city's
streets now that "fucking soldier" Kellen Winslow Jr.
has been dealt to Tampa Bay. You will have to rely on
your nonpareil bottle-throwing skills to protect you.

Dallas Cowboys—The Cowboys were dubbed
"America's Team" by the vice president of NFL Films
in the '70s after he asked Steelers' owner Art Rooney
if he wanted his team to have the distinction and
Rooney refused it. Sorry, Cowboys fans, you were
America's second choice. But if ever there were a vote
on which fan base to wipe from the earth, there's no
doubt Dallas backers would finish first.

Denver Broncos—While other fans struggle with
high elevations, Broncos fans are capable of being
irritating up to ten thousand feet above sea level. The
franchise has been lingering in a rough patch since the
retirement of horsey-faced quarterbacking demigod
John Elway. At last it seemed Broncos fans had a
suitable successor in sulking extraordinaire Jay Cutler.
That is, until new coach Josh McDaniels floated his

name in trade talks, causing Cutler's face to go from sulk to full-on makeup smearing sob. At least Denver fans won't have to invest in a new player's jersey for a while.

Detroit Lions—ABANDON ALL HOPE, YE WHO WORSHIP HERE. The 0-16 season has allowed your team its stake in history, however opprobrious. You're still convinced Barry Sanders is going to return one of these years. When he finally does, he'll be swarmed by a rabid pack of Lions fans demanding answers. He'll run ten yards backward, reverse field twice, fake out six of them, and still get tackled for the prettiest two-yard loss you ever saw.

Green Bay Packers—True cosmopolitans, Packers fans are far too occupied exploring other cultures and expanding their understanding of the world to have any time for football. Just kidding. They're obsessive small-town bumfucks who, though they are traumatized by the very mention of Brett Favre, long for the Gunslinger to return to Wisconsin to be the godfather of all their children and eventually run for governor, only to occupy the position long after his rotting corpse decomposes in its seat.

Houston Texans—As the team's name suggests, Texans fans are an awfully creative bunch. When the city received an NFL franchise again in the early 2000s, citizens were stymied to come up with another mascot. NASA is based in the area, but the Rockets have that covered. What else is there, other than immense sprawl and inescapable gridlock? Oh, right: Texas! Run with that.

Indianapolis Colts—In an odd coincidence, no fan base has perfected the jersey-tucked-into-khaki-pants look quite like that of the Colts. At the same time, no other team's fans own as many of the dreaded shirseys (a T-shirt made to look like a jersey). Following the lead of recently retired head coach and fundamentalist Christian Tony Dungy, Colts fans try to run down at least one gay person en route to Lucas Oil Stadium.

Jacksonville Jaguars—Congratulations! You're the first-ever Jaguars fan! Hopefully that doesn't mean you live in Jacksonville. Should that be the case, the person reading this book for you should have the tact to skip this entry.

Kansas City Chiefs—Like so many others, you've been victimized by the postseason choking tendencies of Marty Schottenheimer. You thought that would leave an indelible scar on you, but then Herm Edwards showed up and showed you what true inadequacy was all about. With Edwards now recently departed, Matt Cassel and Todd Haley have arrived to usher in a new era of crushing disappointment in K.C.

Miami Dolphins—There are two types of Dolphins fans: retirees who need OnStar to reach the stadium and cocaine dealers who try to move product in the parking lot. For those looking at getting back into the weed game, Ricky Williams probably has a good connection for you.

Minnesota Vikings—Vikings fans take issue with observers who mock the Bills for being historically inept in championship games, when in fact the Vikes are also 0-for-4 in the Super Bowl. That's ridiculing that they deserve too. Damn your East Coast bias! That's the last time they share their lutefisk with you.

New England Patriots—You really like white players in skill positions. I mean, you *really*, really like them. But you're also deeply respectful of the Patriots' proud history, which extends all the way back to 2001, the year when most Patriots fans believe the franchise was founded. The sight of a prematurely purchased 19-0 shirt brings you to tears, as does any mention of David Tyree or Bernard Pollard.

New Orleans Saints—Even years after Hurricane Katrina's devastation, there's little chance for you to return to your former home or rebuild your tattered life. But everything's all *bon temps* because the Saints went to the playoffs that one year after they fixed the Superdome. And you got Reggie Bush! He's quite possibly the best back ever to average three yards a carry.

New York Giants—A curious dichotomy separates Giants fans. On one hand, there's the parking-lot-dwelling, car-smashing Jersey contingent that seems to be the more representative of Giants fans in the eyes of the nation. On the other, there are self-obsessed, moneyed Manhattanites who use football games as an opportunity to unleash their inner asshat, then return to their privileged lives in which they deride the Jersey fans for acting like animals. Nonetheless, Giants fans operate under the ridiculous notion that their fan base is somehow classier than that of the Jets, when they share not only the same stadium, but the same territory and many of the same annoying qualities. You do, however, know not to cram your gun into your sweatpants.

New York Jets—You are either one of the guys goading women to flash their tits near Gate D at the Meadowlands, or you are one of the chesticle-flashing women themselves. There are no other types of Jets fans.

Oakland Raiders—Your soul is the express property of Al Davis (those season ticket forms have some tricky legalese), and he may do with it what he pleases. And he pleases to hack away at it with a halberd, the one that he's hung onto since his years ruling over Middle Earth. It's not so bad—at least you get to wear some cool spiked shoulder pads.

Philadelphia Eagles—Ever the environmentally conscious fans, Eagles fans have found a green-friendly way of disposing of used batteries: throwing them at opposing fans, opposing players, stadium concession workers, security officials, Santa Claus, Eagles players who perform badly, and Donovan McNabb regardless of performance. It's important because batteries are kept out of landfills (where they can leak mercury into the earth) when they're lodged in someone's cranium.

Pittsburgh Steelers—People may not understand your need to carry soiled yellow towels and dance awkwardly to polka music, but then they know better than to cross the teeming horde that is Steelers Nation, a phenomenon which, because of flight from economic distress in Pittsburgh, exists in great numbers virtually everywhere on the planet. Steelers fans, when sober enough to be cognizant of their surroundings, drive cautiously around anyone riding a motorcycle, lest they cause further damage to their franchise quarterback. Known for their thunderous chants of "Here We, Steelers, Here We Go," they can also be identified by their constant cursing of the foul day Steely McBeam flounced into being.

San Diego Chargers—You miss the days when the Raiders were based in Los Angeles. Sure, it's still a heated division rivalry, but it's lost the added charge of proximity. Plus, back then you only needed to drive two hours home—instead of eleven—with a silver-and-black-handled switchblade stuck in your kidney.

San Francisco 49ers—I made sure to double-check my Big Book of Regional Stereotypes, and being a denizen of San Francisco must mean you're almost certainly gay. This makes '80s nostalgia somewhat problematic for you. On the one hand, the 49ers were in the midst of a dynasty. On the other hand, it was the height of the AIDS epidemic. I guess that makes it kind of a wash.

Seattle Seahawks—The trusty moleskine pocket journal of the Seahawk fan holds the preciously written narrative of his inner tumult. Words like weltschmertz and anomie crop up a few dozen times. It is half-filled with frenzied, nonsensical tirades about Super Bowl XL, with the rest consisting mainly of recipes for vegan polenta and Sleater-Kinney lyrics. Even when they cheer, it sounds as though they're crying.

St. Louis Rams—You welcome any distraction during the months when baseball isn't in season and you find hockey to be, well, hockey. You'd be much more inclined to pull for the Rams if only the NFL Shop would allow you to order a team jersey with Pujols on the back. And by that, I mean the Cardinal first baseman's name and not actual poo holes. Those you must cut out yourself.

Tampa Bay Buccaneers—Though the pewter uniforms have brought a reasonable degree of success, and even a Super Bowl title, you secretly long for the sherbet orange duds of yore. Sometimes, late at night, you envision a moonlit stroll on the beach with Bucco Bruce. Just make sure he removes the dagger from his teeth first. That thing is not the greatest bedroom accessory. That feathered hat, however, is another story. Tickles the balls in a most pleasing way. Uh, at least that's what I hear.

Tennessee Titans—You're among the best in the league in mobile meth lab tailgating. Which would come in handy if you attended any Titans games. But that would interfere with a life spent entirely outside Neyland Stadium, whether or not the Vols are playing. A shame, because Kerry Collins would drink your whole tailgate under the table.

Washington Redskins—As perennial Off-season Champs, the Redskins dominate the headlines between the months of March and August for their daring and, more often than not, extravagant free agent acquisitions. These free agents are typically of the faded decrepit sort. A recent history of this continually not working out for the best does not deter the Burgundy and Gold faithful from proclaiming that each of these signings (2009's foolishly bloated new contract: Albert Haynesworth) signals a return to glory for the 'Skins. Those fans who don't cheer on the emptying of Dan Snyder's checkbook are sure to be mauled by Snyder lapdog Vinny Cerrato.

II.3 The Memory of Your Team's Epic Playoff Loss Will Set the Tone for All Your Future Personal Failures

Your favorite team will scar you. By that, I don't mean minor emotional fissures you can bury beneath your everyday troubles. I mean deep-seated emotional scars that only manifest themselves in crying jags after premature ejaculation.

For every fond football memory, there will be countless

others that make you retire to the broom closet to weep and curse your creator for your unshakeable emotional dependence on your favorite team. It stands to reason that each year there can only be one Super Bowl champion, meaning the fans of the other thirty-one teams, no matter how positive a spin they try to put on the outcome of their season, are mired in disappointment and despair. That's a lot of suffering. That's even more Valium.

Most fans find a way to handle it, to push the pain down so deep into the recesses of their minds that it only reveals itself as message board vitriol and sublimated aggression toward busboys at chain restaurants. For those who can't, it's an eternity of reliving events that were never in your control in the first place. That guy sitting on the street corner mumbling about Jackie Smith can tell you all about it. It's re-creating the offending memory in a video game and finding no satisfaction when you simulate a different outcome, knowing how hollow and false it is.

II.3.A THE MOST EPIC CHOKES

An epic, gut wrenching loss can lead to a lifelong complex that forces you to push aside your mommy issues and trace blame for all of life's stumbles to that fateful day. The sad truth is that there is no way to avoid this. You chose to become a fan and will accept the emotional degradation that comes with it.

Take, for instance, these epic big game bed-shittings

that have wreaked havoc on the psyches of fans over the years.

Wide Right—The list of Bills memorable postseason failures is long and illustrious, though none are more iconic than Scott Norwood's missed field goal at the end of Super Bowl XXV. Buffalo, of course, went on to lose the next three Super Bowls, none of which were close, meaning this proved to be the Bills best chance at an elusive championship. Norwood played another season then retired to become a real estate agent, which is a lot less interesting than a transsexual murderer bent on revenge. Thanks for distorting our expectations of reality, Ace Ventura movies.

Laces Out—January is the cruelest month for Tony Romo. And December ain't much better. Yup, the Cowboys haven't won a playoff game in thirteen years. In a 2006 playoff game, the Cowboys were attempting a gimme 19-yard field goal that would have won the game over the host Seahawks, but the star quarterback botched the snap and fell short of the goal line after he tried to run with the ball, thus handing the Seahawks a victory and touching off a dazzling series of late-season Cowboys collapses that have brought endless joy to the masses.

Red Right 88. The Drive. The Fumble.—The postseason woes of the Cleveland Browns can be

summed up in three handy phrases, all under the
rubric "Epic Fail."

1992 Houston Oilers—The Oilers led the eventual
conference champion Bills 35–3 at one point in the
third quarter of a wild-card playoff game, only to drop
the game in OT. The franchise would return the heartbreak seven years later as the Tennessee Titans (the
relocated Oilers), pulling off the Music City Miracle
last-second kick return to beat the Bills in the wild-card
round en route to an agonizingly tight Super Bowl loss
of their own. Yes, there's plenty of pain to go around.

Super Bowl III—The Baltimore Colts were 18-
point favorites against a Jets team from an AFL league
nobody took seriously, featuring wildly sideburned
quarterback Joe Namath, who was just beginning to
cut a drunken swath of destruction on vaginas across
the nation that continues to this day, though now more
often with sideline reporters than Farrah Fawcett. The
oddsmakers didn't learn their lesson about the AFL,
as the Vikings were 12-point favorites the following
year and fell to the Chiefs in Super Bowl IV.

1990s Chiefs Teams—The Chiefs had the
second-most wins of any team in their conference
during this decade, clinched home-field advantage
twice, and failed to make the Super Bowl even once.
Both times they held the top seed in the conference
during the '90s, they lost their first playoff game.
Even Joe Montana and Marcus Allen couldn't get

them over the hump, thus illustrating the other-worldly potency that is the Chiefs' failure juju.

1998 Vikings—It's not that the Vikings were defeated by a vastly inferior opponent. The victorious Falcons, at 14-2, were only a game behind Minnesota in the standings. The choke comes when you factor in that Vikings kicker Gary Anderson had his only missed field goal of the season, which would have won the game in regulation. A shame, as this turned out to be Dennis Green's best opportunity at getting his ass crowned.

2001 St. Louis Rams—The Greatest Show on Turf came in as defending champs and 14-point favorites against a Patriots team coached by Bill Belichick that was somehow remotely likeable. Because this was the first Super Bowl after 9/11, people made a big deal about a team named the Patriots winning. Because people are mawkish and simpleminded.

18-1—Undefeated juggernaut New England Patriots (or Greatriots, as their fans would tell you) beaten by Eli Manning. Or rather, the Giants dominant defensive line, but a Manning has to get credit for everything.

There are but a few ways to deflect this mental anguish before it claims dominion over you. Unless you have the option of buying the team and chucking all the offending players and coaches, it's always going to be an indirect kind of relief. There's the always reliable reassurance that your team will be back next year. It's the great loser standby, a mantra necessary to repeat to yourself when it becomes evident that your team has no real shot at a title, but you need to believe the next season holds the promise of great things to come, when in fact it's a total crapshoot at best.

In truth, the only way for this pain to ever subside is for your team to win a championship. Once that happens, all the accumulated torment from years of coming up short is neatly washed away. Unfortunately, the acquisition of this title may take years, if it ever happens at all. Hell, nearly half the teams in the league have never won a Super Bowl.

Until that day arrives, any number of strong sedatives should keep you from nose-diving off the tallest building you can find. Matt Jones can recommend a few.

II.4 Choose a Player to Idolize Based on His Carefully Crafted Public Persona

Selecting a player to idolize isn't anywhere near as significant as finding a team to worship, but it certainly makes things easier with the all-important jersey purchasing process. But worry not, fanboys. Once you do finally land on a team, there are many personality types from which to choose.

Obviously, the type of player who appeals to you is somewhat subjective. It doesn't necessarily have to be your team's best player. In fact, last year ESPN conducted a poll asking fans to pick the greatest player in the history of each franchise, and Ravens fans chose Matt Stover. The fucking kicker! Fortunately, not everyone is as mentally deficient as Ravens fans, so there's probably a good chance you won't fall head over heels for a player who could get pushed around by the water boy.

The dynamics of a team dictate that there are a number of vital personality roles that must be filled. Do you like the big hitter who jars the ball loose from the defender and stands astride over his downed enemy? The defensive end who has trouble leaving his aggression on the field? The flashy receiver with the elaborate touchdown celebrations and the endorsement deal with BlackBerry. His e-mails indicate that he sent them to you from the end zone!

The Stoically Prickish Leader—Possessing an odd combination of a stiff upper lip and a massive ego, he is the face of the franchise. As such, he makes a big deal of dutifully watching nearly as much game tape as Ron Jaworski and overriding the head coach's decisions. When this pays off, he's fawned over by the media endlessly. When it doesn't, he's often seen glowering on the sideline and throwing teammates under the bus to the press. If you love athletes that endorse all the products you buy, he's the one for you. (See: Peyton Manning.)

The Media Darling—From what your TV tells you about these guys, you'd think they pissed rainbows and shat unicorns. A negative word will never be uttered of the media darling by a studio analyst or play-by-play announcer. If this player does, in fact, commit a blunder, the broadcasters will fall over themselves to soft-peddle and explain away the mistake. You'll adore the media darling if you're one of those people who uncritically digests whatever the media tells them, which is pretty much the entire country. (See: Tom Brady, Brett Favre, Tony Romo.)

The Meast—So named for the late Redskins safety Sean Taylor, who was described as a half man and half beast, the meast is an athletic whirlwind, the player who is simply far and away better than anyone else on the field. The only downside to the measts, if there is one, is that as people they aren't terribly interesting. They never really get in trouble on or off the field, never issue any headline quotes. They just go out and dominate. That can be kind of boring sometimes. (See: Adrian Peterson, Brian Westbrook, Michael Turner, Larry Fitzgerald.)

The "Scrappy" Player—A white guy who plays a position usually dominated by black players (receiver, running back, defensive back) with a modicum of success. Lauded for his "deceptive speed" and his supposedly indefatigable spirit, the scrappy player makes up with mainstream media support what he lacks in natural talent. Patriots fans wish their entire team was composed of these guys. If you're a big fan of Elvis, the Rolling Stones, and rap-rock, you'll love the scrappy player. (See: Wes Welker, Kevin Curtis, Reed Doughty, Zach Thomas, John Lynch.)

The Quiet Religious Type—Always eager to preach the lessons of humility and service to God over what occurs on the field, the quiet religious type can be a real buzzkill. But at least he usually keeps it to himself and chooses to lead the life he wants rather than haranguing others, though he will be quick to credit the Lawd for a key victory. It's important to distinguish the quiet religious types from the overbearingly vocal religious ones, such as Ray Lewis, who use the language of faith to draw attention away from a rather homicide-heavy past. If you're keen on Jesus, you're keen on these guys. (See: Kurt Warner, Jon Kitna, Troy Polamalu.)

The Loudmouth Douchehard—Part douche, part blowhard. If you ask me, the title is pretty self-explanatory. The loudmouth douchehard loves to talk shit, whether it's to the media, his opponents, fans, homeless people, the infirm, heads of state, the elderly, or really any sentient being capable of being offended. Any objection to this behavior is interpreted as a sure-fire sign of disrespect, which only leads to even sharper increases in douchebaggery. (See: Philip Rivers, Joey Porter, Jeremy Shockey.)

The Snarling Intimidating Badass—Unlike the loudmouth douchehard, the snarling intimidating badass doesn't have to shoot his mouth off to scare the people on the other side of the ball. A naturally terrifying dude, he oozes quiet intensity. And is probably coated in an enemy's blood. You never really hear from him, probably because reporters are too intimidated to stick a tape recorder in his face. This guy is too tough for you to like him, so step the fuck off. (See: James Harrison, Mike Sellers, Albert Haynesworth.)

The Linemen—Ah, the men in the trenches. They're the most important players on your team that the fans have no clue about. They do the dirty work and yet you'd be hard pressed to find a single person in the stands who wears the jersey of even the best lineman in the league. However, the problem with having a lineman as your favorite player is that it makes you look like a pretentious cocksnot. See, the majority of fans know the linemen are important but it's a tacit rule that they can't be your favorite player. Just live with it. (See: That big fat guy, the one next to him, and the other three.)

The Dirty-Playing Dickhole—This is the player fans of other teams will express the most contempt for, but it's the guy on your team you tend to like the most. Because every great team needs a brutish enforcer, someone who's willing to go above and beyond in order to inflict the maximum amount of pain on the opponent. Everybody loves a villain, especially if he's on your side. (See: Rodney Harrison, Terrell Suggs, Hines Ward, the Broncos' offensive line.)

The Emotionally Unstable Trainwreck—The gridiron can exact a heavy toll on even the strongest of minds, so naturally it totally reams the weak ones. These athletes have a tough time handling the grind and have the occasional breakdown, suicide attempt, or abrupt name change. Should that appeal to a normal person? Probably not. But allegedly normal people don't exist, so who cares about them? (See: Vince Young, Terrell Owens, Chad Ocho Cinco.)

The Inscrutable Wackjob—A close cousin of the emotional trainwreck, only without all the messy depression. Their antics are at once bizarre and incredibly disarming. They might don a wacky costume, film a video of themselves belting out a pop hit in their bedroom, or talk about loving a mysterious substance called "construda" or going into "beast mode" on the field. They're liable to do just about anything, and you'd pay to see any of it. (See: Marshawn Lynch, Laurence Maroney, Clinton Portis.)

The Tarvaris Jackson—Every team has a conspicuous weak link, and this guy is it. An opponent's game plan always hinges on exploiting this player, and it works without exception. Of course, all the fans of his own team hate his guts, but he can be quite the hit with backers of other squads. (See: DeAngelo Hall, the Steelers' offensive line, the Broncos' defense.)

II.5 Know Thine Enemies, So You Can Identify Them After Crushing Their Skulls into Powder

More important than knowing who to love is knowing who to hate. All the best sensations of football fandom flow from the life-sustaining waters of schadenfreude and enmity. What can otherwise be a pedestrian game between non-contending teams can be made instantly enthralling with the simple addition of a little undisguised contempt.

As a rule of thumb, you should harbor an active dislike for all the thirty-one NFL teams other than the one you have adopted as your own. Anyone who says they have a "second favorite team" probably has a second favorite creature that they like to have sex with. However, there should be a small handful of teams for whom you reserve your most fervid store of hate. The very sight of these teams' logos or players should invoke murderous urges that would get you jailed forever if you ever acted upon them.

Most rivalries are based on commonsense reasons, like regional proximity or a history of important head-to-head contests. Others don't really make any goddamn sense at all, but are still fun to watch. If you're confused about which franchise is your team's rival, merely observe which team's merchandise gets burned the most in the parking lot of your team's home field. That's usually a reliable indicator.

Not all rivalries are created equal. Some teams are just too boring or mediocre to inspire intense loathing (looking at you, Arizona). Here are some of the more notable grudges around the league.

Washington Redskins–Dallas Cowboys—It's a standard cliché of the Old West, so it might as well work in football, too. Never mind the fact that everybody in the league hates the Cowboys (justifiably so) and that Eagles and Giants fans probably hate them just as much as Redskins fans. It only matters that the broadcasters get to make hackneyed "Cowboys and Indians" jokes about this matchup. Because those never get tiresome!

Chicago Bears–Green Bay Packers—The NFL's oldest and most storied rivalry dates back to 1921, when a meatpacking company employee and a live carnival bear fought each other to the death over a unicycle. In the years to come, it evolved into a football contest between teams named for these two combatants and has thrived ever since. More than fifty Hall of Famers have taken part in the rivalry over the years, and the two teams cannot be mentioned in tandem other than by a stentorian gravelly voice, not unlike John Facenda. The Vikings also intensely dislike both of these teams, but then the Vikings don't win anything, so who gives a sun-dried shit about the Vikings?

Pittsburgh Steelers–Cleveland Browns–Baltimore Ravens—The Steelers and the Browns were mortal

Rust Belt enemies for generations and all was good. Then in 1996 Baltimore stole Cleveland's team. The Steelers smoothly transitioned to hating the Ravens. A few years later, the NFL gave Cleveland a new team. Browns fans still hated the Steelers but they also hated the Ravens for stealing their team and winning a Super Bowl a few years later. Ravens fans, meanwhile, are content to hate themselves both for living in Baltimore and wearing purple camouflage every week.

Baltimore Ravens–Indianapolis Colts—Meanwhile, the people of Baltimore still have an ax to grind with the Irsay family for relocating the Colts to Indianapolis in the middle of the night in March 1984. They'd have much preferred it be done in broad daylight, like many of the drug purchases and murders in the city. If there's anything Baltimoreans hate, it's secrecy.

Denver Broncos–Oakland Raiders—A heated divisional rivalry that's as intense as any other in the NFL. However, since both teams are located in the western half of the country, East Coast bias prevents most of the country from giving a shit.

Houston Texans–Tennessee Titans—One might think this is a rivalry because the Tennessee Titans were once the Houston Oilers. But actually the two teams are in a constant disagreement about whether it's worse to live in Houston or Nashville.

San Francisco 49ers–Dallas Cowboys—These two

teams have met a record five times in the NFC Championship Game, twice in the '70s, once in the '80s, and twice again in the '90s. This rivalry has resulted in such historic moments as "The Catch" and "Remember When Someone Actually Gave a Fuck About the 49ers?"

Indianapolis Colts–New England Patriots—Perhaps the Niners-Cowboys equivalent of this decade, the Patriots beat the Colts in the playoffs in consecutive seasons, two years before allowing the biggest comeback in conference title game history to Indianapolis in 2006. What's more, Peyton Manning holds the lead in endorsements over Tom Brady by roughly 350,000 products, though the gap is closing.

New England Patriots–New York Jets—This rivalry intensified in the late '90s when Bill Parcells defected from New England to coach in New York immediately after taking the Patriots to Super Bowl XXXI, causing the Patriots' frog-throated owner Bob Kraft to accuse the Jets of tampering. A few years later, Bill Belichick, a day after being named the Jets head coach in 1999, wrote his resignation on a napkin (his usual tactic for picking up married women) and later signed on as the Patriots' head coach. In 2006, the Jets named buxom former Patriots assistant Eric Mangini as their head coach. The next year, Mangini outed the Patriots for illegally videotaping other teams' defensive signals. Such fervid drama barely masks the fact that all these teams really want to do is fuck each other. Mangini was recently fired by the Jets, though the teams will undoubtedly find other coaches to swap acrimoniously.

New England Patriots–NFL Rule Book—The NFL has a set of rules by which they would like all their franchises to abide. The Patriots, however, are above your lousy rules, you narrow-assed National Football League. They're going to tape all the signals they want. What're you going to do about it? Sanction one of your most popular, most hyped teams? Then they're going to hack into your computer and identity theft your ass and use your credit card number to buy some sweet pocket bikes, the kind they'll use to ride all over your lawn and chew that bitch up. And, hey, if Rodney Harrison wants to take human growth hormone, he's going to do it smiling while standing in the commissioner's office and peeing on his desk lamp. Four game suspensions don't mean nothing to him. Rules? Pfft. Ain't no rules in our world, Mr. En Eff Ell.

Seattle Seahawks–Referees—Seattle fans, ever since their team's unfortunate and not nearly caffeinated enough loss in Super Bowl XL, have been harboring the notion that referees are somehow out to get them. They decry as much in poems they write in lipstick on their bathroom mirrors and in chalk on the sidewalks of college campuses. You would be wise not to deny them their conspiracy theories, lest they find a way to implicate you.

Philadelphia Eagles–Santa Claus—In a famous

1968 incident, Eagles fans pelted Santa Claus with snowballs during the halftime show of a December 15 season-ending loss to Minnesota. In retaliation, Santa, teaming with Chanukah Harry, has brought nothing but tainted scrapple and heartbreak to citizens of the City of Brotherly Love for forty-plus years. And, oh yeah, no championships. Luckily, they've gone to gifting each other batteries.

Buffalo Bills–City of Buffalo—The Bills are in the midst of an arrangement through the 2012 season that will have them playing five regular season games in Toronto. Certainly this is a source of consternation to the citizens of Buffalo, who'd much rather the Bills be hopelessly mediocre on American soil. Canadians, meanwhile, will be all too content to clap politely no matter how badly the Bills lose. Nothing gets to those people.

Detroit Lions–Winning—The elusive concept of victory has long bedeviled the Detroit Lions, and they don't appreciate it one bit. So the team has retreated into even greater depths of losing just to spite it. Victory, however, is unmoved and sits on a beach somewhere with Barry Sanders sipping cocktails and texting other teams.

Jacksonville Jaguars–St. Louis Rams–Carolina Panthers–Tampa Bay Buccaneers–Arizona Cardinals–New Orleans Saints—These teams are either too new or too inconsequential to have developed any interesting animosity, so I arbitrarily decided they should just hate each other. After all, football without hate is like sex without hate. It's just no fun.

II.6 Bandwagon Fans: Can't Live with Them, Can't Line Them Up and Melt Their Insides with a Flamethrower

They lie in wait for the majority of the football season until a handful of dominant teams emerge from the pack. They then latch like a remora fish onto the one that's getting the most media attention, pretending as though they had been there all along. They can't recall the bad times that other fans have gone through in the past, nor even what happened in the first few weeks of the season. Most likely they won't even know who was on the team the previous year. Each season, you'll see them sporting a different franchise's jersey. Sometimes they even forget to remove the tags. All they care about is repping a winning team. They are parasites in search of victory, needing only a host team to attach themselves to in order to suck all authenticity from the fan base. They are douchebags incarnate. They are bandwagon fans.

No other figure in the football world is more worthy of your contempt. You may hate the fans of rival teams, but they are loyal to your enemy and therefore possess at least a shred of dignity. You'd like to choke them, sure, but probably not to death, just as a showing of respect. The bandwagon fan, however, is a lowly scavenger, a leach, an opportunist who follows the prevailing winds of the day. They seek no quarter and none will be given.

Rae Carruth would be disturbed by what you'd like to do to them.

In the 1970s, they clung to the Pittsburgh Steelers. In the '80s it was the San Francisco 49ers. The Dallas Cowboys had their already painfully obnoxious fan base amplified by the presence of surplus bandwagon fans in the '90s, bellowing "How 'bout them Cowbooooys?" in unison while doing blow off Michael Irvin's playbook. This decade, bandwagon fans have mostly found a home in New England. Can you remember meeting a Patriots fan before Tom Brady showed up? There was that one guy with a Red Sox hat who kind of liked them, but that's about it. Now you can't go anywhere without seeing the goofy disembodied head they call a logo on the back of someone's car. If you drive an ambulance, you should interpret one of these stickers as a "Do Not Resuscitate" sign. And what of Cardinals fans prior to January 2009? Just kidding. There still aren't any Cardinals fans.

Unfortunately, bandwagon fans are a tragic fact of life, and something we will be forced to endure for as long as the game exists, unless of course Congress finally gets its act together and allows us to forcibly sterilize these humanoid rectal warts.

II.6.A HOW TO IDENTIFY A BANDWAGON FAN

This race of netherpeople is so universally despised, they have learned over the years to conceal their identity. Very few bandwagon fans will admit to being bandwagon fans. Attempting to test their knowledge about their supposed favorite team can be a drawn-out, painstaking process. One easy way around this is to accuse all the fans of the Super Bowl champions of being bandwagon fans. This accomplishes two things: it shames the bandwagon filth, and it pisses off the actual loyal fans who deserve to be taken down a peg.

What is the difference between a bandwagon fan and a fair-weather fan?
It's an important distinction. A fair-weather fan can be defined as one who roots exclusively for one team, but only when that team is doing well, whereas a bandwagon fan is free-floating vermin who changes allegiance depending on whatever team is succeeding from year to year. Sometimes even within the same season. They commit the cardinal sin of sports bigamy. Both deserve to be exterminated without prejudice, the difference being that the bandwagon fan's ashes should to be pissed on, then covered with salt so nothing grows in its place. The fair-weather fan merely merits a fatal bludgeoning with a blunt instrument, but you may leave the corpse alone to be picked at by wild dogs.

What should I do if I encounter a bandwagon fan?
Stand your ground. Their first method of attack will be to taunt you with reminders of how many years it's been

since your team last won a title, if they have at all. Remember that they haven't earned the right to boast about anything because they didn't suffer during their team's lean years. They're sickening creatures and their hollow words should have no effect on you. Bandwagon fans are not known to have a pronounced weakness; however, anecdotal evidence suggests that punching them in the dick usually quiets their trash-talking for a while.

My team is on the verge of winning a championship, which has our fan base beset by bandwagon and fair-weather fans. What can I do?

You can start by sucking it up, asshat. That's the price of success. Nevertheless, it's time to play up your true believer bona fides. The proliferation of bandwagon fans among your crowd means your dedication will be questioned by other team's followers. Start wearing throwback jerseys of popular players from the past, carry around photos in your wallet of you attending games as a kid and, of course, show utter disdain toward anyone backing your team who came to the party late. And nothing shows disdain quite like wrapping someone's body in a carpet and beating them about the face with a replica helmet.

I'm a Chiefs fan and therefore constantly on the brink of suicide. Wouldn't I be better off being a bandwagon jumper?

No. Certainly you have been dealt a bad hand in life. No

one deserves to grow up as a Chiefs fan. But that's no excuse for fanhood apostasy. At the end of the day, you have to be able to look at yourself in the mirror. Don't fall prey to the temptations of cheap shortcuts to glory.

But what if you're a Lions fan?
Yikes. I suppose exceptions can be made.

2.7 Choose Your Friends Based on Football Allegiances—and Maybe Their Parent's Beach House

By now you've succeeded in picking a favorite team. Unless, of course, you picked the Bills, in which case all you succeeded in doing is consigning yourself to a lifetime of misery. Nevertheless, you've made your pick. Congrats. Now you're going to need some friends, if for no other reason that you don't wind up dying unloved and alone like Rick Mirer.

There are several important qualities one should consider when choosing friends at a young age. First and foremost is that your prospective friend won't snitch you out for your gambling pools. Secondly, that they not be one of those football-hating mutants that make the outside world the joyless near-uninhabitable place that it is (we'll cover them in all their loathsome detail later). Beyond that, there's always loyalty, shared experiences, compatible personalities and that other piddling crap you can hear all about on the Hallmark Channel.

Of course, don't discount the wholly valid option of

choosing someone who owns the best stuff. You'll find that disagreeable people with big screen TVs are much easier to get along with than those without. And don't worry if you have nothing to give in return. Half the reason people get great stuff is so that they can show it off to peers. By exploiting them, they're really exploiting you. They should buy you a beer.

Looking exclusively for friends who share your favorite team is another intuitive move. But it's the wrong one. Variance of team allegiance among friends is a highly underrated asset. It heightens the quality of humorous shit talking, which is the foundation of any lasting human bond. Who wants a social group composed of entirely supportive people? If you and your friends are not constantly busting each others' balls, what's the point of interacting at all? Having said that, don't go and do something nuts like befriend a fan of a direct rival. Those are the type of relationships that only end with knife fights on rooftops. Ultimately, at the center of every good friendship exists a powerful undercurrent of resentment. Having friends who like different teams also means your buddies probably won't try to nab your team's players for his fantasy team, allowing you to make all the regrettable homer draft picks you want.

Sooner or later, your two teams will be forced to play one another. This makes for tense times. It also makes for tantalizing bouts of gambling. Though fanhood is a many splendored thing, one of its few downsides is its power to act as a blinding force in making wagers. With its influence, one will always overestimate the fortunes of their team. Even if your boys are clearly inferior, it shouldn't be difficult to get your cocky friend to grant you the Vegas line. If it seems unlikely that your team can even cover that, then it's time to dip into your psychological bag of tricks and question his manhood until he spots you three touchdowns.

That doesn't mean you should go out of your way not to have friends who pull for the same team. Far from it. Instead, space them out. After all, you're going to want a season ticket holder in your social circle to mooch off of. Ideally, this would be the person who you befriended for the kickass TV. Simplifies the ol' contact list on the cell phone.

Don't think it's all big screens and roses, however. Friendship doesn't come without sacrifice. Unless you are Jared Allen or Leonard Little, once in a while you will be entrusted as the designated driver for your chummy chums. This is an important responsibility, likely of life-or-death significance, and one, naturally, you should try to get out of whenever possible. The question is how. This might be the one instance where finding an acquaintance who doesn't like sports or drinking comes in handy. Though phoning a cab could keep you from muddying the friend pool.

II.8 Learn to Deal with People Who Actively Dislike Sports While Somehow Resisting the Urge to Strangle Them

It may come as something of a shock, but there lurks a puzzling breed of people who don't much care for football. Oh, it's true. Some even go out of their way to actively avoid it. And then there's an even smaller, sinister, possibly terrorist subset that hates sports entirely.

As a matter of course in a warped time, you will be forced to interact with these people on a regular basis no matter what it is you do in life. In some cases, you will be compelled to get along with and trust them. You may even have one in your own family. But make no mistake, these people are diseased and should be regarded as such. Because of the baffling restrictions imposed by modern-day society, you will not be permitted to physically harm these people, though their every action and utterance screams that you should. Just keep in mind: There is no NFL Sunday Ticket in prison.

The best approach is to simply humor them as long as possible until they grow disinterested in dry banter and leave you alone. Adopt a polite, but disinterested tone. Answer their non-sports questions with a maximum of three-word answers. "Yeah," "okay," "that's nice," and "I don't know" are effective, time-tested examples. Unfortunately for you, you may stumble into a position where a non-sports-fan is your professional superior. They may not understand why you show up Mondays, if at all, wearing sunglasses and blowing the vomit bits out from between your computer keys. And leave work early on Wednesday to prepare for Sunday's game. This is indeed a terrible predicament. If someone has managed to reach adulthood without developing a love for football, there's little you can do for them, so you'd be wasting your time trying to make them see the error of their ways. They're beyond yours or anyone else's help. Regard them as a professional athlete would you, affecting a dismissive air tinged with mild disgust.

Another smart thing you can do is spend as much time around your fellow football fans as possible. This means regular interaction hours during the week and practically every day during the off-season. Don't construe this as a mandate to be close-minded and eschew other forms of culture. It's important to be a well-rounded individual so that you can accuse fans of other teams of being drooling single-minded idiots. Just remember when you're tooling through the museum or art gallery to engage as few people as possible. They're only going to chastise you for wearing a throwback jersey in their hallowed institution of culture.

If all else fails, become a teacher. They seldom work weekends and have much of the off-season off, ensuring they are less often forced to spend time with non-football-fans. Better still, a large quantity of impressionable minds that you can mold to root for your favorite team. Sorry kid, no gold stars for Dolphins fans.

ARTICLE III

The Formative Years of Fandom

3.1 Matriculate into College (So You Can Learn That Word Doesn't Mean Advancing a Football)

Coming in at a distant second to choosing your team is the choice of which university you will be indebted to for most of your adult life—all so that you may have a few glorious years of justified casual sex and alcohol dependency. Play your cards right, and you might learn to enjoy those magical Saturday afternoons of college football, though never as much as Sundays, unless you live in the South.

Your first consideration should always be price. If it's in an area with a low cost of living, booze is probably dirt cheap and plentiful. Again, the South is good for this, if not much else.

Second is how the school is ranked in athletics. If you plan on playing a sport, you probably already have an obsessive parent to guide you (and to accept illicit gifts on your behalf). And by athletics, I mean football and men's basketball. Men's hoops because you need something for the two months following the Super Bowl. Cling to it like the comfort drug it is. It will stave off the horrors of ordinary life, at least a little, until the NFL Draft. Ideally, you can find a school that exceeds in both sports. And that's in Division I, lest you be foolish enough to think any differently. If you happen upon a university with hot girls and nice weather that isn't the University of Southern California, apply without further consideration. Remember: no USC. You do need a soul, after all. And the chance of getting out of debt following graduation.

At the very least, you need a school that is dominant in one sport. And that one sport had better be football. Having to take pride in a championship lacrosse program is akin to a parent gloating about weeks of unsoiled sheets in their children's beds. You're usually safe taking the flagship big state school. Mind you, attending the community college near the state school does not qualify you as a fan of that school. If you're smart and careerist enough to get accepted by an Ivy League school, good for you. Championship fencing has its moments, I'm sure.

One good thing about college football is that it gives you a deceptive sense of how athletes will fare in the pros. That's important information when filling out mock drafts. Another perk, especially if you go to a powerhouse school, is to be able to take credit for opposing NFL teams' star players. You may hate the Patriots, but you can take credit for Tom Brady, having watched him ride the pine at Michigan.

No matter what university you choose, there is a stuffy climate of anti-physicality you must make sure to avoid. Because you can't afford to blow these formative years on things as trivial as comparative literature.

III.2 The Liberal Arts Agenda Against Fandom

Outside the confines of frat row, the world of academia is not hospitable to the fan of pro football. Even humble state schools can contain stuffy social climates largely hostile to the idea of committing precious mental and emotional energy to following a team. Only at community college will you find students and faculty so disinterested in the act of learning that you are able to let your fan flag fly in the classroom and not be met with derision.

Indeed, college is no place to be a NFL fan. But attending is a necessary evil if you want to avoid having a shitty retail job that will make you work Sundays. You'll be shocked how little your professors want to discuss the results of Sunday's games or how many points you need out of your two remaining starters on Monday night to win your fantasy matchup for the week.

And for a place that prides itself on discovering basic truths about the world, college can be a hotbed of dangerous myths and convincing-sounding falsehoods. Talk to any white feminist with dreadlocks in the student union and among the claims you'll hear about our oppressive androcentric culture is the supposed direct link between days when football is being played and spikes in domestic violence and child abuse. Though this claim will be couched in the most smugly righteous tone, it has absolutely no basis in fact, as you'll be hard-pressed to find any study that finds a statistically significant link between sports broadcasts and violence in the home. Nonetheless, you'll be made to hate your penis more than usual for a few minutes.

To be fair to the ladies, they're not the only ones that college morphs into self-serious insufferable lords of pretension. Try to shoot the shit about the playoff outlook with the average dude at the library and you're bound to get the most askance look this side of the high school parking lot you're still scoping out.

Ultimately, it's a two-way street. Football fandom tends to have an anti-intellectual bent, while intellectuals have a bias strictly in opposition to the awesome. This is a divide that needs reconciling. Not that tomes on Heisenberg belong in the stands or people with replica helmets belong in corporate boardrooms. Still, an understanding can be reached. Though a massacre of the gridiron disinclined would produce a raw, animalistic charge, we need people capable of rebuilding civilization after it's burned down in post-title riots. Therefore, let us conclude that football fans can stand to be a little more intellectually rounded. And intellectually rounded people can stand to be down with a few rowdy tailgates. It's all about the breadth of experiences. This is how we're going to strike a happy-clappy balance among all peoples. I can feel it happening, can't you, drum circle brothers? Let's get a quick Namaste.

III.3 Attend a Game a Week and a Class Per Semester:
A Fan's Guide to Higher Education

Football fans really begin to come into their own during the college years. It is then that you learn to structure the social calendar around daylong benders in front of the TV, followed later by hookups heavy with future regret. And to build an alcohol tolerance that will last you a lifetime.

To excel in college—an excelling defined by doing just well enough to skirt by—you have to be able to budget your time effectively. Because Saturdays can be chewed up by time spent with the college game during the day and chatting up slumpbusters in the evening, not a lot of studying gets done. Sundays are a total washout, for obvious reasons. I mean, you could take a crack at getting work done before the early games start, but best of luck with that in the midst of a hangover. Studying with a hangover will give you a nuanced appreciation for how the Bears run their offense.

Mondays will be spent nursing Sunday's hangover. Tuesdays are a nonstarter because of the boozing concentrated during Monday Night Football. That leaves Wednesday as your lone full day of study before the college weekend begins in earnest on Thursday night. So if you're industrious enough to cram a week's worth of work into that brief window, you'll do just fine.

Where college can best assist you in your fandom is with the critical incorporation of boozing into cheering. You may not realize this during your teenage years, but watching the game majorly sucks when you're sober. Especially before an important game, you're a jangly bundle of nerves that feels no relief until a win is secured or defeat is certain. And then what have you to soothe yourself with during a loss or to catapult yourself further into Flavor Country after a win? Getting blackout drunk can greatly ease the nerves and jettison those pesky inhibitions. If you want to be able to remember what happened during the game, well, that's what DVR is for.

For many, tuition might be a hefty price for a lesson in inebriation you could cheaply get on your own. No arguments here. College, like personal seat licenses, is a colossal rip off, one for which the spendthrift and the foolish among us will gleefully shell out. Say, however, you are serious about doing some learning, building a career, and all that claptrap. Then you might want to consider sticking exclusively to spring semesters for enrollment. The fall simply isn't conducive for the football-inclined to get much else accomplished.

III.4 Befriend NFL Prospects Now, While They'll Still Let You Do Their Homework for Them

An understated boon to attending a large state school that doubles as an athlete mill is there's a decent chance that at least one of these players will share PSYCH 100 with you, thus enabling you to supplicate to them shamelessly in hopes of gaining a potentially famous friend for life, or at least until they get their first signing bonus. Play your cards right and you could work your way into their already teeming entourage of hangers-on and extended family members. That's potentially one sweet gravy train.

Being a dude puts you at a distinct disadvantage for the football player's sympathy, as you possess staggeringly low quantities of vagina, leaving them with little motivation to even acknowledge your presence. Proving you're more sycophantic than the rest is gonna take a Smithersian effort of favor-currying.

Do not be deterred by little things like plunging into moral bankruptcy by compromising your dignity at the feet of athletes, at least when it's done in the interests of football. College is the only chance you have for gaining the friendship of a professional athlete. Once they get to the pros, the protective bubble they've enjoyed as athletes all their life gets impossibly insular. Rare is the time they will even have to pretend to interact with the public.

Of course, earning the trust of future NFL players is no small task. They understand that everyone wants a piece of them now that they're on the verge of attaining great wealth and notoriety. Excessive though it may sound, just keep in mind that you could find yourself on the list of fifty friends he gets tickets for when his team makes the Super Bowl.

III.4.A THE DUTIES FOR THE ASPIRING HANGER-ON

Ability to have several jars of your own clean urine at the ready at any point in time.

Limitless capacity for reassurance.

Willingness to place fingerprints on guns, knives, steel briefcases, corpses, stores of uranium, no questions asked.

Personal bodyguard. Or even body shield. (Taking a beating or a bullet gives the athlete precious time to flee danger.)

Facility with telling reporters to fuck off.

Sufficient parenting skills to raise one or more of his illegitimate children and maybe one of his agent's.

A proficiency with Photoshop (to superimpose his face on Batman's body).

A keen aversion to snitching.

Enough writing chops to ghostwrite the biography he puts out during his rookie year.

Promptness in calling the Cheesecake Factory in advance for reservations.

Keeping player's cell phone ring from becoming out of date.

Spamming blogs that report on his misdeeds.

Leveling up his *Call of Duty* online gamer ranking.

Writing threatening letters to Jim Rome.

Acting as designated driver, no matter how much they want to pull a Donté Stallworth or Leonard Little and mow down pedestrians under the influence.

Picking the banana-shaped candies out of his packages of Runts.

Throwing off the public by posting misleading updates on his Twitter page.

Protesting outside Electronic Arts headquarters because of his skill ratings in *Madden*.

Carrier of extra cell phone for when he forgets to charge the first one.

Campaign manager and speechwriter (for post-NFL career congressional run).

III.5 Watch Football While Tripping Balls: Drugs and Gameday

Just as Christianity is its de facto religion, alcohol is the mandated intoxicant of the NFL, despite it being one of the principal causes of the violence among fans that outsiders persistently bemoan. But other drugs can be added to the mix to enhance your viewing experience.

While we hate for our favorite players to get caught with drugs because it leads to suspensions that jeopardize the team's prospects for winning, using them ourselves may add to the gameday experience. With no rigid moral codes in place for fans, we're free to test out any substances we like without fear of public condemnation. Legal issues are another issue. Not having drug charges automatically thrown out because we're not famous is a minor concern, however.

In order to best tailor one, or several, hallucinogens into your gameday routine, it's wise to examine the attendant effects of each drug and, once you've made up your mind, start putting your furniture on Craigslist in order to buy some. Because focus is a necessity, some narcotics are better than others. At the same time, you need something that's going to block out the disjointed ravings of Tony Kornheiser.

Weed—Marijuana, obviously, will mellow your shit. Enough so that everything about the game becomes an enthralling spectacle. Even the playing field itself. The enchanting green. Look at it! So what if someone just ran a 75-yard triple reverse. That's not a green found often in nature. While that's great for games you're not emotionally invested in, the paucity of homicidal rage will, even in your addled state, strike you as inappropriate. Grade: B, because it's a tactile letter.

LSD/Cocaine/Heroin/Crack/PCP—You're not very much interested in watching football if you're taking any of these. Similar things you're averse to doing include holding a job, not stabbing people for spare change, and living to see the next decade. At the same time, these can be appealing alternatives to watching the Raiders play. Grades: LSD: D; cocaine: even though it's a helluva drug, C-; heroin: F; crack: D; PCP: F.

Lean—Unlike the Texans, this drug is very popular in the Houston area. A cocktail of cough syrup, cold medicine, alcohol, soda, and Jolly Ranchers, the ingredients seem as hastily cobbled together as the Chiefs' starting lineup, and are of equally valuable materials. Grade: Heeeelll Yeeeeuh.

Construda—A mystical concoction whose properties are only known to those daring enough to try it and resourceful enough to obtain it, construda is said to be the most potent of fictional drugs invented by Laurence Maroney. Grade: the letter does not exist in the English alphabet.

Speed—Does the game not move fast enough for you, huh? Huh? Doesn't it? What are those people doing? Why are they huddling? No huddle! No huddle! Why isn't there more action? Oh man, the play clock is only at ten. This shit is moving at a glacial pace. I need action. C'mon, let's do this! Grade: B+++ ++++++++++whyaren'ttheremoreplusses?!

Ecstasy/Ketamine/GHB—The game won't make a lick of sense to you, but you'll be awfully eager to give out that celebratory touchdown hug, as well as the lesser known first-down hug, weak-side-run-for-four-yards hug, pass-batted-down-by-a-lineman hug, inside-two-minutes-booth-review hug, and garbage-time-touchdown hug. Grade: K, because it's special.

Meth/Quaaludes/ OxyContin—Welcome to Tennessee Titans Nation! Make sure to keep your meth lab well stocked with nachos and fire extinguishers. Grade: C, because that's as far as you got in the alphabet.

Paint Thinner/Varnish/Turpentine—Even if you failed to poison yourself to death, then you certainly blinded yourself, which is still preferable to watching a game between NFC West opponents. Grade: Backward G.

Booze—Still the standard-bearer of football intoxicants. It helps for yelling but also for hypersensitivity to the most meager slight to your team. Did that guy just clap for the other team getting a first down? Time to introduce his head to the bar railing. Grade: C+, B+ if you're not drinking a crappy macrobrew that gets advertised during a football game.

III.6 Countries Most Likely to Cease Being Useless and Catch Football Fever

With all the regionalism that dominates football fandom (because rooting against another team also means carrying a deep-seated dislike for its home city), one would assume football fans must be wanton xenophobes who have no interest in sampling foreign culture. And unless you're a fan of one of the teams from the AFC South, that couldn't be further from the truth.

There's nothing that exists within the mind of the fan that makes that person resistant to flights of wanderlust. Travel can be one of the finer off-season activities a fan can partake in. Thing is, what would make traveling abroad that much better would be if these misguided, hidebound foreigners would just wake the fuck up and accept that our sport is demonstrably better than anything they have going. It's not much to ask, really.

The phenomenon of football fandom has taken hold better in some countries than others. Some have the potential to be brought around, while others remain defiantly irredeemable. These are things Lonely Planet doesn't bother to tell you. Suppose you're roped into a honeymoon or vacation in the middle of the season? Called out of the country on business? Maybe you still think you can hack it in a country without a football receptive culture. You've got the Internet, after all. And in a large cosmopolitan city, there's bound to be one or two places willing to show the preferred athletic-related diversion of the oppressor. Sorry. Not that easy.

Even with your precious sports bars and Internet, consider the can of worms that awaits: Suppose you find a bar willing to show the game. The broadcast is either at a god-awful hour, depending on your time zone, or it is being shown on tape delay, which forces you to avoid looking up the score on the Internet until it's aired. Make it to the appointed broadcast time, staving off long enough the overpowering urge to look up the score, and marvel at the setup you get stuck with: the smallest TV in the corner of a crowded bar where the other patrons are unconcerned with your objectively most important interests, the bastards. More annoying still are the foreigners who pretend to care about the game you're watching.

Try to keep your composure as they divert your attention from the game with admissions that they don't much understand how American football works and they'd like you to explain it to them. As an American, they don't expect you to be polite, necessarily, though an elbow to the face might skew extreme on the scale of possible reactions.

England—The NFL has tried to push its appeal across the pond, first with the failed NFL Europe, now with annual regular season games in London. Whether that means a substantial uptick in interest from Brits remains to be seen. Given the NFL's paucity of dry wit and advertisements on the field of play, it seems unlikely to take. Eagle fans, however, will feel right at home during soccer hooligan melees.

France—"Please, please, monsieur, the French have no time for your silly game for ruffians. Your continued outbursts are a disturbance to the riveting game of pétanque currently being played by six xenophobic old men in the street. Leave us in peace and go drool on your shoes elsewhere."

Italy—Oh, wow. They have a siesta in the middle of the day, where businesses close and people go home to eat and rest. It's so laid-back, it's like how Randy Moss plays when he doesn't think his team has a shot at the Super Bowl. In Italian culture, the number seventeen, instead of thirteen, is considered unlucky, which should make sense to any Panthers fan.

Canada—Why not just go to an adjacent city? Or a grocery store? For all the difference in culture you're getting in the Great White North, if you're not scoring cheap drugs you're wasting the gas. They do have a football league of their own, in which twelve guys named the Roughriders vie for a title in the Grey Cup, which still sounds like a hockey trophy. They do have a partial stake in the Bills, which is almost an NFL team.

Argentina—The Argentinian penchant for massive beef consumption will surely please any football fan, though the country's mania for soccer and hidden Nazis will not. Convincing residents of the NFL's virtues isn't an impossible task, so long as you can convince them that Diego Maradona is actually the Chargers' Luis Castillo. (Fact: About the same weight.)

Brazil—If you're able to pull one of the insanely hot women the country is famous for, you just might be lulled into swearing off everything you hold dear in your life. That's the danger of visiting a place as seductive as Brazil. That or getting kidnapped and having your organs harvested by a Rio street gang. One or the other.

Netherlands—Gee, wonder what it is that brings you to Holland. The quaint windmills? The undeniable lure of clogs? I think we both know it's the Anne Frank House. And the legal marijuana is nice too. But is that such a huge deal? Is weed really that difficult to acquire in the U.S.? If someone as dumb as Nate Newton can get his hands on more than two hundred pounds of it, my answer would be no.

Africa—Yes, I lumped all of Africa into one monolithic entity, while taking the time to individually list several predominantly white countries. Because I'm culturally biased like that. I had to learn it from somebody. Hurl the charges of insensitivity at society, not me. I love Christian Okoye, but do they? So if there are no study programs in most of Africa, how did you end up there, anyway? That means . . . waita-minnnute! You joined the Peace Corps, didn't you? That entails sacrificing years of your life to help the dispossessed and generally be a force for good in the world. You bastard! Way to make us all feel like selfish assholes. That's self-examination I do not need. It's enough to make me puke.

Russia—Instead of the frozen tundra of Lambeau Field, visit the actual frozen tundra of Siberia. There, you're just as likely to stumble upon something approaching civilization. A dour people, Russians could be persuaded to latch onto perpetually miserable fan bases, like those of the Lions or Bengals.

China—Though the Chinese have little interest in the actual sport of football, they are indeed intrigued by the authoritarian manner in which the league is run. In particular, Redskins owner Dan Snyder is an unlikely popular figure in the country for his success at cramming as many seats into FedEx Field as is physically possible. For a country with a severe overpopulation problem, these are critical management skills.

India—Conditioned to enjoy Bollywood entertainment, the people of India appreciate the choreographed dance numbers that NFL cheerleaders put on. However, at an average length of roughly three hours, Indians find football games far, far too brief for their tastes.

Israel—Dangerous? Absolutely. But suicide bombs can add a dash of Middle Eastern flare to any victory riot. Looming peril aside, football's presence in the Holy Land is on the rise. Patriots owner Bob Kraft recently became the official sponsor of the Israeli Football League, meaning there should be no shortage of cameras to capture the action. Given his success rebuilding the fortunes of his own franchise, Israeli teams should have more fans than the Cardinals, Jaguars, and Texans by the printing of this publication.

Japan—In the Land of the Rising Sun, NFL games start at 1:00 a.m., as Sunday turns to Monday. One might argue that's a small price to pay to be in a country full of vending machines carrying underage girls' panties and tentacle porn. And they'd be right.

Australia—A right stubborn lot, the Aussies went to the trouble of developing their own set of rules for the game of football. Just who do they think they are? Listen, you incredibly lighthearted, charming, sunny people, just because you committed four soldiers to the war effort in Iraq doesn't mean we're going to stand idly by and let you impose whatever perverted rules you want onto the game of football. Some things transcend the bonds of allies, you know. And next time, please send us a slightly less mincy, less-musical-theater-friendly actor to play Wolverine.

III.7 Land a Football-Related Job

Sans extraordinary athletic talent, there's obviously no hope for you making it in the NFL. Somehow that eight-minute 40 time didn't blow away the college scouts when you were in high school. Instead you'll have to plan for another field of work that doesn't require exemplary physical skill. Something like the UFL.

But the NFL can still be a calling even to the athletically disinclined. With numerous professions on the periphery of the sport, being involved with the league in some capacity is within your grasp.

AGENT

Pro: Extremely lucrative profession, though available only to those who've forfeited their soul. Not only encourages but requires you to disregard the internal sniveling nag you call a conscience.

Con: Entails going to law school or getting some other advanced degree in the field of sports management. Must also carry out three mandates of Satan's choosing.

BROADCASTER

Pro: High-profile profession. With the always ballooning size of pregame roundtables, there's little chance you'll ever be unable to find work. The public's expectations of your performance are set very low thanks to the work of your colleagues.

Con: High-shitshow-quotient profession. The steady stream of banalities that one is forced to utter may be germane to the job, but will turn your brain to mush and your heart to a blackened, viscous stew. Worst of all, you may be forced to converse with Joe Buck.

COACH

Pro: Exerting a strong influence over what happens on the field. Your meltdowns in front of the media will be recycled into unfunny Coors Light commercials, possibly earning you royalties.

Con: Having to get your start at some D-III school in bumfuck nowhere. Living under constant scrutiny. Getting approximately thirty-three seconds each year to relax. Basically being unhappy and ulcerous all the time.

REFEREE

Pro: Can alter the outcome of an NFL game in dramatic, controversial ways. Ample chances to make a killing by accepting bribes.

Con: Can be forced to have your mind on matters other than the game. An NFL official is only a part-time job because the league is retarded and wants to ensure none of the referees devote that much time to their profession and are therefore incompetent.

GROUNDS CREW

Pro: End-zone paint is a little-known hallucinogen.

Con: Blame will be heaped on you when clumsy receiver trips over his own feet. Doing your job at Heinz Field is equivalent to being the one man assigned to guard the U.S.-Mexico border.

PRINT JOURNALIST

Pro: Laziness is not only encouraged but rewarded. Interviewing famous athletes is an integral part of your daily routine. So too is gorging at the press room buffet.

Con: You'll be despised, scorned, and likely threatened by those same athletes. Any news you break will never be credited by ESPN. So it's pretty much a miserable existence that will be thankfully truncated when you're laid off in the next round of newsroom staff cuts.

BALL BOY

Pro: It's the next step up from water boy. Allowed to stand on the sidelines and look important, which is about as much as Scott Linehan ever did.

Con: Not so much a career. The job also tends to go to kids. At some point, every ball boy gets slapped by a player. Even Nick Lowery, a kicker, got in on the action once.

ACCOUNTANT

Pro: Bean-counting is so much sexier when the beans are football-shaped.

Con: Issuing audits to companies that improperly use NFL insignias makes you more of a tool than most accountants.

SECURITY GUARD

Pro: Ability to bust skulls with impunity. Only requires a degree in being burly.

Con: You could get stuck on Pacman Jones bodyguard detail.

SPORTS SURGEON

Pro: Manages to be lucrative without all the cumbersome moral baggage that the agent job comes with. Get to stick a knife into Tom Brady's knee free of consequence.

Con: Requires a decade or so of schooling. And always living in the shadow of Dr. James Andrews.

TEAM DOCTOR

Pro: Able to brag to friends that you were the one to give steroids to Shawne Merriman and painkillers to Brett Favre.

Con: Testifying before Congress during steroid witch hunts can be burdensome. Especially if you make the mistake of meeting Charles Schumer's malocchio.

SPORTS PSYCHOLOGIST

Pro: No one really knows what it is you do or whether it's even helpful, but they respect it.

Con: You don't even know what you do.

GUY WHO DRIVES THE INJURY CART

Pro: Affords close proximity to NFL players, if only when they're horribly mangled. Plus, you get to drive a cart. Essentially the perfect job.

Con: Might need some special class of cart license or something.

III.8 Root for Your Team from Afar

Moving to the territory of another team will obviously mean putting up with their fans every day of your suddenly miserable life. Factoring in the expense of the occasional vandalization of your home into the household budget is to be an immediate consideration.

Surpassingly popular teams, like the Cowboys, Steelers, Giants, and Packers have pockets of fans in every market, which goes a long way toward explaining why these fans are universally thought of as the most annoying. You could burrow into the deepest subterranean morlock colony and there'd be a Cowboys fan holed up in there claiming that Michael Irvin never pushed off a defensive back in his life.

The truth of the matter is that every fan base is annoying to those who are not members of it. For followers of the aforementioned nationally prominent teams, convening with their fellow fans is simply a matter of tracking down the bar where they congregate to watch games. Others don't have it quite so easy. In fact, to walk around in a Texans jersey is to be stared at like you were some kind of freakish oddity, as though you were wearing a garment made of syphilitic penises. Which is weird, because everybody knows that's what Bills jerseys are made of.

Since you're now separated from the core of your fan base, any time the team visits your adopted city (or comes within three hundred miles) it's your solemn obligation to make it to the game. They need you to be the drowned-out voice of praise amongst an overwhelming chorus of hate. As you might expect, the experience of the fan at an opponent's stadium is a drastically different one from being at the home field. Bottles of urine will be hurled at you, for starters.

Consider the venue. There are some stadia, stadia located in certain cities in the southeast corner of Pennsylvania, where it is unadvisable to root for the visiting team. Not that it's necessarily bad form, but because you'll be left for dead in a portable toilet and rolled down a hill.

Don't go overboard with gloating. One wave of your genitalia to opposing fans per half should be sufficient—only when your team is ahead, of course. Otherwise it's just garden-variety indecent exposure.

Learn the specifics of the stadium. It's not difficult

to find season ticket holders at any stadium willing to
dump seats to visitors, even for the biggest of games.
That said, there are those who would unsurprisingly
exploit your ignorance for their gain. That means
selling you marked-up seats with a view obstructed
by a pillar. Or planetesimal-sized fans. It's a scumbag thing to do, but you have it coming if you're not
well-schooled on where you're going. So do a little
homework, or push the passed-out guy in the next
row out of his unobscured seats. He won't notice until
well after the game is over. And by then he'll be more
occupied with fishing his face out of the layer of sludge
on the ground.

Careful with the illegal behavior. What you can
get away with at the home stadium is far different than
what you can do elsewhere. There's nothing home fans
like more than ratting out fans of the visiting team, no
matter how seemingly innocuous their behavior. Naturally, the ushers are only too happy to comply with
their demands, not to mention rough you up for their
enjoyment. Concealed cameras on your person are
a boon to your lawyer after you get your collarbone
snapped.

Beware the bathrooms. Other than the parking
lots, this is where the majority of visitor fan beatings
take place. So I would recommend not using them at
all. Pissing yourself may be the greatest defense you

can employ against the savagery of the opposition. Who wants to get close enough to a guy reeking of urine to clobber him? Streaks of feces under your eyes also send a message to potential inflictors of pain.

ARTICLE IV

The Two-Minute Driven Life

IV.1 You Can't Have a Tailgate of One

The human mind, conditioned over the course of millennia spent enduring without football, is hardwired to seek out the comforting presence of others. It made sense to need people when humankind was floundering aimlessly in search of purpose. Neighbors, friends, and loved ones provided welcome relief to the existential crisis that wracked a sports fan without a real sport.

With football now discovered and flourishing, the elusive purpose has been found, yet our dependence on the acceptance of others lingers. We could perfectly exist on our own with our TV and our shrines to our favorite team, content to interact with other fans only on gameday. A shame that we remain victims of an outmoded primal urge that one day evolution will hopefully expunge. Until that day comes, we are bound to deal with our cumbersome need to belong.

Satisfying this biological need entails a circle of friends, presumably of the drinking-buddy sort, maintaining at least tenuous relations with our relatives and, because the species demands it, finding a mate and starting a family. Anyone can tell you it's far more work than it's worth, but you really have no say in the matter.

The rigmarole to starting and keeping these relations in place is a trying one. Among the tedium you're facing down are the tasks of getting an education, holding down a respectable job, and keeping a good faith effort at personal hygiene. Some part of every fan would be content to be the bum with a bottle of booze sleeping on top of a warm grate. But society dictates that this is not an acceptable lifestyle, and before long, you will want to feel embraced by your peers. That, and among the homeless it's getting increasingly difficult to stake out a good vantage point near storefront TV displays come kickoff. You've got to be on your game about that.

In the end, it's a lot to put yourself through for what amounts to be a great deal of aggravation most of the time. The people in your life will give you hell, but on some level, you're going to need them around. The social circle isn't all bad, after all. It helps to have a support system in place for the times when your favorite team falls tragically short, or even more miserably, nowhere close, and you need someone to talk you back from the ledge.

Now if you could only get one of them to make a goddamn beer run for you. And get out of your face for three hours a week.

4.2 Make the Game Part of Your Game:
Picking Up Women

There's no drunken hookup like a random celebratory football fan hookup. Both man and woman are feeding off emotion, wanting to extend the high of a win or mollify the low of a loss. And people naturally become more attractive if they're fans of your favorite team.

Some fan bases are more attractive than others. A fan of the Jaguars, Packers, Vikings, Ravens, Texans, Rams, Steelers, Lions, Colts, Titans, or Browns? Then the pool of attractive ladies among your crowd is pretty thin. The odds aren't working in your favor. But then, beggars can't be choosers. Or so they say. Nevertheless, don't despair, no matter how many times you may be striking out. It makes you look meek, which translates to tragically undesirable in a football crowd.

Football, of course, is a team sport, and so too is hollering at chicks. Both require intense calculation, a high threshold of pain and ass-slapping. The first among your needs is a quality wingman, whom you are free to consider your lineman. Or your blocking back, depending on what kind of offense you're trying to run or which you consider less homoerotic. That wingman must excel at occupying the edges, picking off any of the friends protecting your desired woman's blindside. If your wingman can also lie really convincingly on your behalf, you might want to give him the franchise tag.

Given a clear shot at your target, bring forth the full

force of your charms. Draw from the same well of energy you use to get drunker and louder during the playoffs. If you won your fantasy league title last year, now's the time to let her know. Women respect success in all its forms. Did you recently place high in a *Madden* tournament? You should keep a few screenshots of final scores in your wallet. Good as pussymagnets, those.

Though this interaction is offensive in nature, you must be defensive in temperament. The picking up of women is like the delicate dance between a defensive back and a receiver. You must think of yourself as the cornerback. You try as best as you can to keep up with receivers, anticipating their moves, pressing them off the line and back into the bar, all the while making sure not to make contact before the time is right. Strike too soon and you'll draw a flag, which in all likelihood manifests itself as a kick to the balls.

Many times you will be called upon to be a wingman yourself. You are part of the team after all, and any carry you get is countered with time spent on special teams. Be prepared to give up your whole body for the cause. You're springing your man for a score. All you had to do was get pancaked by a three-hundred-pound defensive lineman, or, more literally, the three-hundred-pound friend of the targeted girl.

It can seem so intimidating, this sordid little routine. Luckily, Internet dating can be an attractive alternative to this *danse macabre*. Best of all, Internet dating is quickly losing its stigma as a refuge for the awkward and the ugly.

That means one thing for you: searching diligently for women wearing your favorite team's jersey in their profile picture. A tattoo of the team logo is also acceptable. Like information on a team's roster, facts can be embellished in your profile. If elfish receiver Antwaan Randle El can be listed at five foot ten, there's no reason you can't list your income as "over $250,000."

Should you succeed in sealing the deal, celebrate in a manner not unlike you do after a team score, replete with "good game" ass pats and spilling beer on her. Then give a wide berth to the girl you hooked up with at the bar for the remainder of the season. Good as fandom lays can be, relationships can seldom take bloom in that setting. Before long you find the intensity rarely matches the energy that first drove you together. Or the drunkenness.

4.3 Convenient Conditioning for the Football Fatty
It's no secret that the sedentary, gorging lifestyle of the average football fan isn't the healthiest to which you could subject yourself. Minus a concerted effort at proper personal care, the constant ingestion of greasy food and the endless supply of alcohol—all done while sitting on your ass—could turn a healthy, svelte individual into Jared Lorenzen in the span of only a few months.

Caring about one's appearance has commonly been derided in fan circles as the mark of the effete, but it's important to have self-respect. Especially for trash-talking purposes. A fan base full of lardasses opens itself up to easy mocking from the supporters of other teams, not to mention endless inquiries as to whether they plan on finishing a food item.

Moreover, as much as unwatchable sitcoms on CBS may have convinced you otherwise, you can't be a slovenly mess and hope to attract a good woman who puts up with you. No, you've got to put forward a modicum of effort to keep yourself semi-presentable. That or become obscenely wealthy. Your call.

Should you decide on fitness, a few simple strategies, easily incorporated into your regular sloth-filled routine, can produce dramatic results.

For every six regular beers you drink, have a low-calorie one. It'll trick your metabolism into thinking you're trying to lose weight, thus kicking it into high gear. Either that or the horrible taste will make you swear off drinking for a round or two.

Hide the remote. No, it won't force you to get up and change the TV manually more often, but it will force you to yell for someone else to do it. And yelling has to burn at least a few calories, right?

Eat work-intensive foods like crab legs or sunflower seeds. They require so much effort, you'll think of eating as a chore and won't want to do it at all. That is, unless some enterprising merchant is selling sunflower nutmeat. Then you is screwed.

Stop eating your weight in bacon paste. It's probably for the best. And not just because your heart stopped pumping an hour ago. Your resulting gas will also melt the eye membranes of those nearby.

There is no such thing as victory cake. Neither is there first-down cake. Nor blocked punt returned for a touchdown cake.

Don't pee into a soda bottle. Getting up once in a while to visit an actual bathroom burns fat and is a much more sanitary option. At the very least find a large bush. Sure, peeing into the bottle saves time and provides you a projectile to chuck at a Titans fan, but it's disgusting. And likely causing you to put pee-soiled hands on your other food articles.

Limit yourself to one pound of wings per quarter. Any more than that and you're talking more hot meat injections than Jeff Garcia.

For every lineman who scores, waddle in place for five minutes. If one fat guy can move his ass for a little bit, surely you can do the same. You can even reward yourself with some jumping-jacks cake after you're finished.

Gastric bypass surgery. No one said you had to do it the honest way.

Utilizing these small measures, you'll keep yourself from becoming an unsightly amorphous blob, instead staying a charmingly paunchy glutton. No one wants the clap of their thighs to overmatch those of their hands.

IV.4 The *Diner* Quiz for a Post-Post-*Diner* Generation

The 1982 Barry Levinson film *Diner* is best remembered for the scene in which a young man gets his girlfriend to touch his penis by concealing it in a popcorn box at the movies which later served as the inspiration for the Justin Timberlake and Andy Samberg song "Dick in a Box" (as seen in that movie with Daniel Stern).

A more critical segment for our purposes occurs later in the film when Eddie, played by Steve Guttenberg, subjects his fiancée, Elyse, to a rigorous examination of her football knowledge. Nothing much, just 140 or so questions on arcane gridiron facts. Elyse hangs tough, but in the end finishes with 63 percent correct, falling just short of the 65 percent mark required to pass. If this strikes you as draconian, you clearly married out of desperation, intoxication, or on a dare. Maybe all three. Gauging the football acumen of a potential mate is an all-important determinant in the courting process. Otherwise, your betrothed may be a concealed non-sports-fan, one who has merely cannily constructed a clever façade until the ring gets on her finger. You'd be stuck. Maybe even for months before the divorce was finalized.

That said, *Diner* is a Hollywood movie and, as such, gets several critical details glaringly wrong. For one, quizzing football fans on stats and trivia is a largely pointless tactic. Stats are only important insofar as they can help our fantasy teams. Slavish reliance on statistics for sports enjoyment is the realm of baseball dorks. It's all they have.

Without statistics, baseball would have nothing but the overbearing crush of nostalgia and wacky mascot races. And if they could quantify nostalgia, they'd get Bill James to create a stat for it in a heartbeat.

Football, on the other hand, is chiefly about emotion, often frighteningly intense and wildly erratic emotion. That's why you must craft your test on personal experience over objective truths. This may seem to feed into the perception that football is not as intellectually stimulating a sport as others, but that ignores a categorical fact: FOOTBALL'S JUST PLAIN AWESOME, DOUCHECANOE. WOOOO!

Therefore, asking her for descriptions of the first game she attended, how she became a fan, and the most painful loss she ever experienced is more revealing and instructive than whether she knows which college some random player attended. If you're concerned that such queries will be more difficult to score, fear not.

IV.4.A THE FOOTBALL MANIFESTO MATE-MATCHING METRIC

The first order of business is figuring out where you're going to conduct this examination. Any number of forbidding, intimidating venues could conceivably work, though there's a certain amount of jolting verisimilitude to setting up a table on the 50-yard line of a high school football field and having friends, acquaintances, coworkers, and ex-boyfriends fill the stands. Or, you know, if you want to make it racy as opposed to clinical (the NFL would not approve), you could always opt for an actual classroom and her in a naughty schoolgirl outfit. One thing *Diner* got right was the refusal of bathroom breaks during the proceedings. The last thing you need in a significant other is someone who's going to drag you out of your seat during a two-minute drill. Unlike in the movie, you should be as generous as possible with any water she requests. You're really going to want to test that bladder. A nearby slowly dripping faucet is a nice touch.

In many ways, you have to look at this like it's a football tryout. Most football players who reach the NFL have the physical attributes to excel. The same is true with potential spouses. It's character issues that determine who flies or falters. If you've gotten to this point, you should have some sense of what the person is like in the sack, so that needn't be part of this examination. Besides, once you get married, you won't be getting laid anyway, so you might as well figure out how much suffering you should expect beforehand. Consider this the wifely Wonderlic.

A composite score will be produced based on performance in eight football-pertinent fields:

1. Trash-talking: Demand she write a thousand-word essay on why hers is the best team in the league. If that team is not your own, immediately dock her points. Score for creative use of invective and cheap slurs. If she writes in all capital letters, you probably met her on the Internet. If that's the case, just be happy a woman showed up.

2. Passion: Insult the starting quarterback or head coach of her favorite team. Immediately provide her with a mannequin. Time her on how long it takes her to dismember it. Anything over twenty seconds isn't marriage material. Impose five seconds of penalty time for each eyeball not gouged out. Remind yourself to never do that again.

3. Patience: Sit her down for a conversation with Chad Ocho Cinco. If she can stand his nonsensical musings for five minutes, she's willing to deal with anything.

4. Appearance: You know what's hotter than a girl who knows a lot about football? How about one who's just hot? Sacrilege, I know, but the last thing you want to end up with is a female Packers fan. Sure, the various cheeses she feeds you will be delicious, but good luck peeling a woman the size of Gilbert Brown off you in the morning.

5. 40 Time: Clock her time in the 40-yard dash. This shouldn't factor into your decision, but it will probably be fun to watch.

6. Pink Jerseys: Does she own one? If so, run. Now! Stop reading! Move!

7. Punctuality: Request a beer. You may be in the middle of a field with no refrigerator in sight, but the truly dedicated will find a way around this. The average commercial break is about two minutes, so make this your cutoff time. Anything over that mark is an automatic fail. Ditto if the beer she brings you is a Coors Light.

8. **Is She Actually Submitting to This Test?:** *Diner* was a movie released in the '80s that was depicting life in the '50s. Women were considerably more subservient in those days, so much so that they might actually put up with a bullshit exam like this. Women ain't having it nowadays, playboy. So if you find one willing to undergo this charade, it probably means she loves you. Just marry her already, you dumb fuck. Like anyone else is going to put up with you.

IV.5 The Obligatory Guidelines for Female Fans

Women have made startling progress in football fandom. So much so that the definition of who is a football fan is quickly and dramatically changing. Football, more than any other major sport, has long been considered the province of the penile persuasion. Women, so went the conventional wisdom, would never be interested in a sport where people violently flung themselves into each other, or at least one in which Oprah didn't play a prominent role. However, with each passing year, more women have proven their bloodlust is as strong as that of men. The road to female fan proliferation was not an easy one, especially considering how much of the language of fandom is so heavily cloaked in misogyny. Male football fans often express their disapproval of a player or a rival by calling that person a "bitch," "pussy," "pussybasket," "crotch pheasant," "twatblossom," "cockwallet," "fucktaster," or another such term of endearment.

If you're a female fan, you're bound to get harassed a

few thousand times per game. Unlike baseball fans, who are polite to the point of dithering, football fans aren't shy about obnoxiously and drunkenly coming on to you.

Sensing the groundswell of new female fans, the NFL has tried to capitalize on the boom in several only marginally patronizing ways. A number of franchises hold football clinics for women to teach them the basics of the game, which is an asset for women whose boyfriends or husbands don't like them enough to teach them things. Taking it a step further, in the summer of 2007, the Baltimore Ravens started a fan club specifically for women called Purple. The most prestigious members of Purple are known as the Lavender Ladies, which is something so mind-bendingly tacky it could only exist in Baltimore, or possibly Green Bay. Of course, much to the consternation of Ravens fans of any gender, the team with the highest percentage of women in its fan base is the rival Steelers, because apparently women can't get enough of waving kitchen towels around.

That isn't to say female fans don't still struggle for acceptance. Some gripe that men are intimidated by women who unabashedly possess a profound understanding of and keen insight into the game, fearing that if a woman knows more than they do about football it somehow undermines their basic manhood. Well, yeah. Sure it does. But there's a decided upside too. And that is that men need female fans. Why? Because any unhealthy fixation for men is suddenly made socially acceptable when women find it appealing.

IV.5.A GROUND RULES FOR FEMALE FANS

Don't wear pink jerseys.—Ever. That the NFL sells them
is an affront to your dignity. At best, they can be worn
ironically by male fans as a means of mocking a player
who is considered preening and fey. Someone, like,
say, Tony Romo. But for women it's a definite no-no.

Don't be overbearing about your football acumen.—
You know you know a lot about football, but you want
everyone else to know it too, so you feel the need
to force your expertise on other fans all the time.
Women can't be faulted for this insecurity, as it's
the result of pigheaded men who refuse to believe
women know sports. Still, feeling the need to prove
yourself at all times is unnecessary and grating. Say
a guy questions how you could possibly understand a
Cover 2 defense. Don't waste your breath explaining
how Tony Dungy's version gets all the credit though
it really originated with the Pittsburgh Steelers
schemes in the 1970s, when you could just punch him
in the dick. So much easier, so much more amusing.

Don't adopt your boyfriend's team.—I won't be so
rigid as to say you aren't allowed to date—or
even marry—outside your own fan base, but for
God's sake, don't adopt the team of your new boyfriend. Don't you have any self-respect? You're
your own person. To do so smacks of craven
codependence.

Don't say rival players are cute.——If you're a fan of the Colts, it's your duty to say you don't find Tom Brady attractive, even if you do. If you're not thoroughly disgusted by every player who's not on your team, you're liable to swap your baby for a cuter one in the nursery. You monster.

Use the language of the oppressor.——There's no better way to take the power out of misogynistic language than by using it yourself. That's called reclaiming, but it's also called being funny. So go crazy! Call a guy a bitch. Tell opposing fans to suck your dick. See how empowering that is? Admit to the book that you're turned on.

Don't be surprised that even if you do everything right men will still shun you.——The fact remains, many male fans see football as a male-bonding time or at least a respite from women, especially the married ones. It is not wise to deny them this as it will only cause problems. This is why homes should have at least two HD screens. If Mr. Man needs his alone time with the pigskin, even if you like to watch, you can act like giving it to him is a big deal. That's a great bargaining chip.

IV.6 Vow to Have a Football-Themed Wedding

Mazel tov! You actually found someone. Marty Schottenheimer wants to know how you closed the deal. It's no easy feat. Most of fankind has trouble keeping the TV tuned to the same game for an entire quarter, let alone putting up with one person for decades at a time.

If you have come this far and she still doesn't like football, you're going to have to rethink this whole thing tout de suite. Single life isn't so bad if it means unfettered access to the Sport of Sports. By the time you hit your mid-forties, you'll be having as much sex as the married guys anyway. And there will be no one to stand in your way when you turn your one-bedroom apartment into a veritable team shrine, replete with game-worn player underwear obtained on the black market and nailed to your living room wall.

But if she can at least tolerate your lifestyle you might as well go through with marriage. And what better way to jump into this eternity than planning a football-themed wedding? Blowing it off and eloping in the Caribbean? Sure, but you can't afford that.

First thing's first, as first things often are. When is this big matrimonial mishap gonna go down? Planning it during the football season invites a clusterfuck of Raiderlike proportions. Good luck finding a weekend when everyone's team is on its bye. With a seemingly limitless number of weekends to fill between mid-February and August, you'd be a fool not to go for the spring wedding. Plus you get a ceremony complemented by the enchanting efflorescence of the season, and everyone knows football fans really get off on that shit.

With the spring wedding date set, an outdoor event is definitely the call. In football, teams that play in a dome are always perceived as weak because they never are subjected to the elements. The same applies to people who get married indoors. The mettle of your relationship is not tested. The thing could fall apart by the first snowfall. That's why you need an outdoor ceremony. (Sweeping generalizations borne out by limited history form the backbone of all football discourse, so let's roll with it.)

The trappings should be obvious to any football fan: bride and groom enter through giant inflatable helmets, the guests sit on bleacher seats, the priest/minister/rabbi/officiant is decked out in a referee's uniform, the bride comes out to "Crazy Train" by Ozzy Osbourne, or Zombie Nation, depending on whichever you find amps up the crowd more effectively.

Upon arriving, each guest should receive a jersey. Just like NFL rosters, the numbers should be assigned according to position. Anyone who arrives after exceeding the ninety-nine available spots will be placed on waivers and can be acquired by another reception.

1-2: Bride and groom

3-9: Parents, siblings, minister/rabbi/nondenominational referee

10-19: Close friends, mentors, the person no one likes who gets number 13

20-39: Extended family, local baker with whom you share a close relationship, running backs and defensive backs

40-49: College roommates, AA sponsors, ex-girlfriends/ex-boyfriends

50-59: Assorted single people, Joey Porter if he accepts your invitation

60-79: Coworkers, neighbors, Laotians, random people with interesting jobs

80-89: Wedding crashers, children born out of wedlock, cousin who "ain't right in the head"

90-99: Catering staff, chef, bartender, the one fucker who just had to have 95 THANKS FOR BEING DIFFICULT, FRANK!

Once the guests have been seated on the home and visiting sides, the processional and opening words can commence:

Minister: "Dearly beloved, we are gathered here today in the sight of Goddell and these witnesses to join number 1 and number 2 in matrimony, which is commended to be honorable among all men; and therefore is not by any to be entered into unadvisedly or lightly, but reverently, discreetly, advisedly, and solemnly. And definitely not without an adequate supply of wings. Into this holy estate these two persons present now come to be joined. If any person can show just cause why they may not be joined together, let them toss their red challenge flags before the next snap is taken."

The bride and the groom will present the exchanging of vows.

Best Man: "ARE YOU FUCKING READY? THIS IS IT! RIGHT NOW, RIGHT HERE, WHERE ELSE WOULD YOU RATHER BE? LET'S DO THIS SHIT!"

Bride: "YEAH!"

Groom: "C'MON! LET'S GO! LET'S GO! IT'S OUR TIME!"

Bride: "NO ONE CAN TAKE THIS FROM US! NO ONE CAN TAKE THIS FROM US!"

Groom: "LET'S TEAR THE ROOF OFF THIS BITCH!"

Bride: "I'M ABOUT TO RUN THROUGH A FUCKING BRICK WALL!"

Groom: "AAAAAAAAAHHHHHHHHHHH!"

Bride: "AAAAAAAAAHHHHHHHHHHH!"

Minister: "And now the presentation of the rings."

Groom: "I give this ring as a symbol of OUR COMMITMENT, DAY IN AND DAY OUT, TO PLAY TOGETHER AS A UNIT, NEVER TO STRAY FROM THE AIMS OF THE WHOLE, AND TO PUT YOUR FUCKING GUTS ON THE LINE EVERY TIME YOU STEP OUT OF BED IN THE MORNING."

Bride: "And, to you, I offer this ring as a symbol OF FUCKING SHUT UP FOR SIXTY MINUTES, TO NEVER HAVE AN OUNCE OF QUIT, TO

*BREATHE FIRE AND SHIT NAPALM FOR AS
LONG AS WE CAN PUT ON THE MOTHER-
FUCKING PADS!"*

*Minister: "By the power vested in me by the
American Football Conference, the National Football
Conference, and the Office of the Commissioner of
the National Football League, I now pronounce you
husband and wife. You may exchange flying shoulder-
butts in a celebratory fashion, on three."*

IV.7 Raise Your Kids to Root for Your Team
Through Coercion

In football, as in life, you need a game plan. Nowhere in
that game plan should there be anything about getting a
woman pregnant, in or out of wedlock. It's not part of the
scheme I've careful and meticulously laid out for you. I
can offer you little in the way of advice on getting out of
the mess you're in. There are no audibles here, unless you
know how to game a paternity test. If you do, there might
actually be a future for you in the NFL, though not necessarily as a player. More likely as a "consultant." Not able
to scam the test? Then welcome to the suck. What you're
faced with is not all that different from a team trying to run
out the clock when they're down big and ready to cut their
losses. Except instead of sixty minutes, you're gonna need
to run off sixty years. Sorry, no new life is coming next
week. That said, there's still no excuse to shed your parenting game face for your little bundle of wonderful. At least
until it's eighteen.

But if you've gone and done the deed, buck up, sulk monkey. Most of your favorite professional athletes have the same problem. Only they have money to pay someone else to raise the kid—or, as is more often the case, kids—for them. As a father, your job is not dissimilar from that of a coordinator to a domineering coach: stay out of the way, let your spouse make the big parenting decisions. That way you can reap the benefits when things go well and avoid the limelight when they don't. Granted, a co-ordinator stands to gain a possible head coaching job of his own, while at best you avoid complete destitution and possible public humiliation. Again, life can't be as enjoyable as football. That can't be stressed enough.

If you need a player comparison, think of yourself as an impressive-looking but ultimately useless decoy, sort of like Reggie Bush, only you're not banging Kim Kardashian. Though it's possible you may already have.

Your primary objective for the next few years is to coax your child into adopting your favorite team. It's the only shot you'll have at developing any affection for the little soul sucker. To accomplish this goal, no means should be considered off-limits. Blackmail, psychological programming, idle threats, real threats, locking him or her in the towel closet for weeks at a time. Don't consider yourself a parent. You're officially an envoy working on behalf of the team. Any failure on your part will be the gain of a competing team. Then you're only empowering the enemy, making yourself not only a weakness but a liability.

With the kid on your side, expensing those season tickets

becomes significantly easier. Yes, you have loads of other expenses that go unaddressed, but you're not being selfish by spending inordinate amounts of money on a needless hobby, you're bringing a hint of joy to your child's otherwise drab existence. Which makes you immune from spousal grief. And one day that child will grow up and become your designated driver. Or, if you push them obsessively enough, a crazed professional football player incapable of emotional connection. But one that will make you fabulously wealthy. That almost sounds like a plan.

IV.8 Acceptable Levels of Involvement in Your Kid's Pop Warner League

Not having risen to achieve athletic stardom never caused you much distress. You knew you had neither the skill, the determination, nor the freakish genetics necessary to make a push at a pro career. Sure, you dabbled with high school ball a little, but it wasn't much more than an attempt to appease your blowhard of a father, who demanded you strive for the heights that he himself could never reach. That, and if you didn't join the team there was more than a fair chance you wouldn't have gotten laid until midway through college. Girls aside, you vowed never to be like the overbearing father figure who forced that grueling game upon you. You were going to be a cool parent who allowed his kids to make their own decisions and host parties and smoke cigarettes and even join the goddamn forensics team if that's what they wanted.

But that was until you had a son of your own and that open mindedness went the way of your hairline and youthful whimsy. Now you stare at that amorphous blob of afterbirth and wonder if he will ever amount to anything more than an Xbox savant who weighs three hundred pounds at age fourteen. That little shit can bring you a reflected form of the gridiron glory you never got on your own. Did you see the way he leveled that kid at daycare? He's the next Justin Tuck.

The warning signs of the pushy sports dad are obvious. Leave them unchecked and soon you'll be the next Marv Marinovich, the former NFL player whose hard-line parenting tactics raised a failed robotic first-round pick quarterback of a son. Marv went as far as having a football in Todd's crib from the day he was born and having him teething on a frozen kidney.

Maybe you won't be so extreme. Still, you must exercise restraint. Do you find yourself forcing a macrobiotic diet on the kid once he gets off the bottle? "Candy only gets him off his regimen of pain!" Step the fuck off, buddy. What you think is instilling an early sense of discipline is only building resentment of you. With those tactics, you have a better chance of turning the tyke into a serial killer than a football player. And Dexter's dad already made the blueprint for that.

What if the kid decides to play of his own accord? Don't take this as a sign to go batshit crazy and run wild with your obsession. Stick with restraint. Act like this is just another passing interest he's chosen to take up before shucking it all off in favor of heavy narcotics. Your job is to show up at the games, voice support when appropriate, and otherwise keep your fucking yap shut. And for crap's sake, don't try to coach the team or give the coach advice about getting your kid into the game.

Your children will find myriad ways to disappoint you that have nothing to do with sports. Leave it to them to decide what those towering embarrassments will be. Given some space, there's less chance they'll freak out and become members of the American Taliban pushed into domestic terrorism because they were forced to pore over playbooks instead of watching cartoons like a normal seven-year-old.

And, hey, if you strike the offspring lottery and your kid does wind up an NFL superstar, you're going to get credit whether you compulsively impelled them toward it or not. So sit back and roll the die. At least that way you can spend more time boozing.

IV.9 Scenes from a Broken Fan Marriage

You really think you know somebody. Years of Sundays spent together glued to the couch in matching Elway jerseys watching the Broncos do battle. She'd even wear the white horsehair wig to complete the look. It one was of the few moments of honest kinship you ever felt with another person. Two souls, joined forever in marriage and fandom. And afterward joined again for some postgame play. It was a beautiful thing.

Wasn't it just a few months ago that you got her a new authentic Kyle Orton jersey for her birthday? It was a message to her that, in addition to being the foundation of your past, she represented the reality of the present and the promise of the future. The mother of your children, the source of all ardor, the chick who didn't mind when you ralphed in her hair when you first met. It was a gesture pregnant with symbolism. It was a present that cost three hundred goddamn dollars.

Of course, she took it to mean that you thought she, like Orton, had a neckbeard.

Bitch.

It was then you should have figured it out, but you remained willfully blinkered to the truth, to her conniving nature. The morning your buddy Nick took you aside and said he had spotted the wife in a Darren McFadden jersey in a bar with another Raiders fan, you refused to believe it. You even lashed out at Nick, saying that was a vicious canard that only a Cowboys fan could spread. What a fool you were. He was only looking out for you.

You wouldn't even address the allegations. You didn't ask her. Then she came to you and said she had to go out of town the weekend of the Broncos-Raiders game in Denver to attend the wedding of one of her work friends. Since when would she put anything above a rivalry game? Fishy as it was, you let it go.

But then you noticed she didn't pack any of her Broncos jerseys for the trip. Surely, even at a wedding, she could slip out come kickoff and find a place to get rowdy and watch the game. There were no two ways about that with her.

When she got back from the trip, you asked about the jerseys, trying not to sound too leery. She laughed it off as a freak mental lapse, maybe in a little too facile a manner. Shouldn't she be more frustrated about that? The woman you'd always known, always loved, would have been. That more than anything piqued your suspicions.

It wasn't many weeks or many more attempts at subterfuge before you finally cottoned onto her game. The tips from friends became more frequent, more detailed, more embarrassing. She became more brazen about it, not even bothering to say why she was heading out on gamedays.

You'd had enough. Cobbling together the info your friends gave you, you found their bar. Less than two miles from your home. *Your* fucking home. There, planted right in front of the TV showing the Raiders-Chiefs game, was the wife. She was looking every bit like a one-woman Black Hole. She saw you as soon as you walked in the door and shot you a wry little smirk, like you finding out didn't mean shit to her. It probably didn't.

It was just then that her newfound guy made his way back from the bathroom. You could tell he recognized you, seeing the flash of fear register in his eyes. Maybe she showed him a photo. Maybe it was 'cause you were wearing the Elway jersey. You didn't even ask the guy's name, but man, you beat that silver-and-black ass like you were Steve Atwater.

'Course, with your brutal outburst, there was no way you were getting sole custody of the kids. Oh, your darling son Terrell Davis Henderson and your radiant daughter Shannon Sharpe Henderson. How you'd give up anything for them. Well, anything non-Broncos-related.

The split custody couldn't have worked out any more in your favor. You got Tuesdays, Wednesdays, Fridays, and Saturdays of your choosing. You'd never miss a single game while she'd get stuck babysitting on every day the NFL's active. More than a little poetic justice in that.

Not as much as the fact that the kids stay true to Broncos Nation. They do their daddy proud.

IV.10 Lord Your Personal Success Over Baseball Fans Because You Don't Spend All Your Time Watching Baseball

A key advantage to football fandom, one that has no doubt helped spur its proliferation to world conquering levels, is that it's not that huge a drain on the viewer's time. Suppose that you watch no sporting event other than your favorite NFL team's games. That's a commitment of a mere three hours per week during the season. Assuming they don't make the playoffs, that's only forty-eight hours per year. Two measly calendar days. The average guy spends more of his time going to town on his crotchular regions.

Meanwhile, the baseball fan commits ten times as much of his life annually to following his beloved stickballers. Five times if it's basketball or hockey. I can't speak to the time commitment to the lesser sports, though I would peg each hour spent with them to be the visceral-thrill equivalent of a clock-killing kneel-down in the NFL.

Followers of these sports would argue that this indicates that the football fan is less dedicated than they, that ours is a fandom of convenience. The football fan should not be guilted into the Sisyphean nightmare that is perpetually following a grueling sport that breeds only boredom and softies. Simplicity is an ideal to aspire to. That football fans can spend less time on their sport and be relatively slaked in their thirst for competitions means they are achieving satisfaction with an economy of effort. As people who eat low-fat food have to consume more to fill themselves up, so too do baseball fans have to fritter away greater portions of their lives to achieve a minimum of excitement.

Not that the football fan wouldn't take more time with his favorite sport if he could, but the sad fact is that it simply isn't feasible. As we've seen, entrepreneurial spirits have tried to fill the empty months with Arena Leagues, CFLs, and XFLs (and soon the UFL) and immediate families, but it's not good enough to maintain our attention.

With the free time that football fans are given, they are primed to lead rounder, more successful lives than their lesser sport counterparts. Sure, market research indicates that on average NHL fans make more than NFL fans, but that's only because one of the two hockey fans in the country is exponentially wealthy. The other is Elisha Cuthbert, who is hot, so we cut her a break.

Free time is one thing when you're young with time to burn, but as a married man, you're lucky if you can squeeze in a few sanity-sparing moments to yourself. Football in these years is the respite that keeps you from walking out on your family. There's no chance you could, with wife and kids, maintain a hard-core never-miss-a-game fanhood with a baseball team even if you wanted to. Which is probably why those whom you spy as regulars in MLB parks are fellows who look as though they make love to their scorecards.

Football is the sport for adjusted people with real priorities, like taking kids to soccer practice and a host of other shit people don't really want to be doing. Football understands the strictures of modern life and doesn't impose excessive time commitments on its fans. If inclined, you can blow just about all the time you want during the season on following all the up-to-date news on your team and the rest of the league, but football gives its casual fans the opportunity to keep up without sacrificing their entire lives. Even when that's exactly what we wish we could have, year-round and without commercial break.

Gameday Operating Procedure: The GOP That Wants You to Have Fun

V.1 Flout the Fan Conduct Policy

In a ham-fisted response to recent negative press reports detailing the nasty, horrible, no good, very bad behavior by fans at NFL games, league commissioner Fidel Goodell last year spelled out a brand-new fan code of conduct policy that forbids just about anything that makes unruly fandom worthwhile, such as drunk-and-disorderly behavior, the use of abusive language, or even lighting shit on fire. Why not just take our grilled meats while you're at it?

This is a disgusting overreach of authority by a still relatively new commissioner trying to consolidate his power. First Goodell made a statement with his severe disciplinary rulings against ne'er-do-drive-sobers such as Chris Henry and Adam Jones, but now he's overstepped his bounds by messing with the very lifeblood of his league:

its fans. A word of advice: Don't poke the bear, rich fortunate son of a senator.

Some aspects of the policy make sense. Any fan already knows not to interfere with the progress of the game without someone having to put it in writing. Trying to conflate that general guideline with the act of throwing objects on the field is where it really starts to get sticky. That's just misleading. You can totally bombard players and coaches on the sideline with objects without it affecting anything on the field of play. Browns fans do it all the time!

Naturally, the league seeks to engender a more family-friendly environment to further spur revenue gains by getting more kids and uptight morally righteous asshats in the gates. But maybe it's not the league's fans who need to change. Maybe it's families that need to sack up. When was football ever intended for them? You know what, families? Everything in our cultures feels the need to cozy up to your inoffensive, anodyne standards, but some of us want cringe-worthy violence, unprintable language, and nudity for miles. Football is something cathartic and restorative for people forced to be polite and civilized against their will 340 days a year. We need an outlet for low-grade anarchy, lest it spill over into society at large. Deprive us of that and suffer the consequences.

Because the NFL conveniently leaves the enforcing of its draconian fan rules up to each team, there are a few interesting wrinkles around the league. The Tampa Bay Buccaneers, for example, instituted a program whereby thin-skinned dickbags could tattle on people having a good time by texting stadium officials to report supposed wrongdoing. While you may think taking advantage of this feature makes you in compliance with the fan conduct policy, it also puts you in direct violation of the fan misconduct policy against snitching laid forth in this book, making the violator subject to a prompt sewing up of their butthole. The NFL cannot possibly enforce these restrictions without fan cooperation, and it's our job to ensure that that never happens.

Enforcement of stadium behavioral policies is nothing new, which makes this policy all the more infuriating. The Eagles have, for years, had a jail cell and a judge inside their stadium for severe transgressors, which creates a curious dichotomy with all the amateur executioner fans they have. But this new policy is a blatant attempt to create positive spin for the league, which was never exactly struggling to get people in the stands. So why fix what ain't broke? Because monkeying with effective practices is one of the more unfortunate traits that runs through the NFL. Just look at how Brad Childress refuses to use the run effectively.

If the No Fun League wants to bite the hand that feeds it, it's time for that hand to bitch-slap the league right back in its dirty whore mouth. How's about this: fans as citizens rise up and support measures banning owners from bilking states and municipalities out of public funds for stadia. Does that sound good, you billionaire cheesedicks?

You pay your own way for the fucking stadium your team plays in eight times a year, and we'll make sure to behave appropriately in it. Until then, choke on our dicks.

Having said that, there's not a hot dog's chance on Wade Phillip's plate that that will ever happen. So perhaps the way fans can have their voice heard is by just buying fewer tickets. Considering how much greedy owners want to charge season-ticket holders for personal seat licenses, this may not be the worst thing in the world. And you know what? You can pretty much be as verbally abusive and blitzed as you want at the local team bar. Why, with the way the NFL wants to hem in the ways fans can enjoy the stadium experience, with its overpriced beers, poor sightlines, and heinous traffic, the dirty secret about NFL fandom needs to be definitively put forward: that it's much better to watch the games on TV anyway.

V.2 Personal Seat Licenses Are a Bigger Rip-off than Buying a Home

Now that the housing market is dicked and the nation's economy is in the crapper, at what other moment could fans be more receptive to forking over more cash for the right to purchase tickets? I write in reference to the ever-infuriating phenomenon of the personal seat license, a one-time cost, usually in the thousands, which entitles the owner to the right to continue paying for season tickets each year until another stadium is opened and the cost is charged again.

PSLs aren't a new phenomenon, as they're believed to have been around for about twenty years, but they've been brought to the fore with their ever escalating costs. The reason cited by sports organizations as to why they impose these outrageous fees on consumers is that PSLs supposedly offset the expense of constructing stadia, many of which are already paid for in large part by tax-payer dollars. Are fans demanding venues that cost squillions of dollars? Not really, but that doesn't stop owners from launching into a space race against each other for bigger and higher capacity venues. The owners opt for these leviathans then pass the cost on to the fans. The gall is as astounding as it is predictable.

When the Giants and the Jets move into their new $1.3 billion shared stadium in the Meadowlands in 2010, every seat will require a PSL for the Giants and nearly every one for the Jets, with the PSL fee for a few thousand spots in the lower bowl of the stadium reaching as much as $25,000 per seat. The Jets auctioned off 620 PSLs of choice seats in the new stadium and drew more than $16 million for the winning bids. Of course, a fair percentage of those bidding for seats are companies in the business of reselling tickets, which only extends the daily chain of corporate fleecing of the average fan.

About half the teams in the league have policies that require PSLs. That's half a league ready to dry-hump their fans for the sweet release of the green. Why anyone would allow themselves to be fleeced by these organizations, no matter how much you may love their product on the field, is beyond the bounds of reason. Fandom knows no quit, but it does know a shit deal when it sees one.

Imagine the hubris that gives rise to these policies. In what other business can companies force a membership fee on customers only for the right to purchase their product? Demand for the NFL product being what it is, the owners think they're insulated from the cost of alienating a wide swath of their fans, but there's only so long, especially with the looming threat of uncapped player salaries, that these practices can continue without it starting to chip into the all-important bottom line.

The fan experience in the live event is increasingly becoming the providence of the superwealthy and the superprofligate. The new generation of stadia that's been built in the past decade crams more seats in and, with prohibitive prices, marshals loud die-hard fans further from the field. Watching the game on TV is not without its flaws (e.g., Phil Simms, Chris Berman, Tony Kornheiser), but it is certainly a much better value than paying through the nose for attending a game where fans are fleeced on concessions, limited by infantilizing fan conduct policies, and generally treated like unwelcome houseguests in overbuilt plutocrat strongholds.

The practice is an insidious money grab devised by billionaires looking for bailouts on their own risky business endeavors. If some fans are economically secure enough that it isn't a bother for them, great for them. But the owners may find that, in tougher economic straits, there will not be as many people comfortable doling out tens of thousands of dollars for the privilege of being bilked on an annual basis. We may love our teams, but that doesn't mean we need to love their scams.

V.3 Your New Pair of Underwear Is to Blame for a Ten-Loss Season

Though a great many hard-core fans insist on using the pronouns "we" and "us" when discussing their favorite team—as though they too suited up and helped block for extra point attempts on gameday—their influence on what occurs on the playing field is limited to little more than the occasional false-start penalty.

This, of course, is one of great fallacies of spectatorship (right along with the notion that analysts' power rankings actually mean anything at all). Fans have everything in their lives arranged in accordance with a set of rigorous conditions that they believe promotes success, which, in other words, equals whatever happened the last time the team won a game. This micromanaging, though off-putting to outsiders, can be the difference between a win and a loss.

Unfortunately, there are no hard-and-fast rules to go by in establishing a proper set of superstitions, such as genuflecting at doorknobs while wearing your Tom Brady Underoos. You have to work through some trial and error before stumbling on the perfectly orchestrated pregame routine that works best for you.

Once you discover your winning formula of OCD-esque ticks to perform before each game, you must never deviate from it. Everything you do is part of a karmic and behavioral pattern that determines who wins on Sunday. It's your duty to your team to obsessively re-create the conditions of whatever happened during your team's last win. And not just on gameday. It extends for the full week prior to gameday. Week 1 is particularly difficult, as its run-up begins when schedules are released in the spring. That's an entire summer of preparation for one game. No wonder that opener is so fraught with tension.

But what happens when you remain completely faithful to your superstitions and your team still loses? This leads to a moment of wrenching soul-searching on the part of the obsessed fan. Indeed, you must examine which of your rituals have lost their luck-inducing qualities and must be jettisoned immediately. Do you need a wholesale change or slight tinkering? All will be revealed the next time your team produces a win. But with each loss comes more and more indecision until running stark naked through traffic to the stadium sounds like a good idea. You'll see that a lot at 49ers games. The best solution is just to label other people in your personal life as bad luck.

The Jinx

The same energy you reserve for adhering to your arsenal of effective superstitions should be applied to avoiding the dreaded jinx. You cannot jinx a rival team, but you can hurt the fate of your own by doing little more than forgetting to use "if" as a preface before discussing the consequences of your team winning its next game. That's all it takes. Jinxes take root in the fertile soil of hubris.

It gets worse; jinxes can originate from forces extraneous to the fan base, leaving fans scurrying to counterbalance the bad energy with forced humility. For example, a prominent columnist or network football analyst, someone who doesn't have any direct involvement with the game, can jinx a team by assuring the public that there is absolutely no chance that it can lose. And, being the fools they sometimes are, members of your team can, by appearing on or sponsoring certain products, create a jinx that morphs into a curse. These are the most notorious:

The Sports Illustrated *Cover Curse*

The *Sports Illustrated* Curse condemns players or teams that appear on the magazine's cover to immediate failure or disgrace. Most likely both. Though it is the most infamous and longstanding of product-related curses, it has lost some of its potency in recent years. This is due in part to the fact that *Sports Illustrated* is a shell of its former self, meaning the curse could still be intact but, because no one bothers to read the thing, few people notice.

The Madden *Curse*

The gold standard in modern individual curse-inducement. Look at some of the players who have graced the cover of this video game franchise that sells annually in the millions: Michael Vick (went to prison), Daunte Culpepper (career ruined by knee injury), Shaun Alexander (career ruined by sucking), Donovan McNabb (suffered a sports hernia the season that he appeared on the cover—I hear that causes pain in your sports back), Ray Lewis (failure to meet murdering quotas in three of the following four years), Vince Young (fell into depression because he couldn't spend all his time hanging out shirtless with dudes). And most recently Brett Favre (who led the league in interceptions and missed the playoffs, despite extensive media fellatio). Frankly, it's unclear why any NFL player would subject himself to such highly jinxable conditions. Unless the rumors are true that these people do really enjoy large sacks of money.

The Chunky Soup Curse

Less celebrated than the *SI* and *Madden* curses, but no less debilitating. Like the *SI* curse, it results in failure on the field or personal injury. For instance, Steelers quarterback Ben Roethlisberger appeared in an ad for the soup and won a Super Bowl, but months later made Chunky Soup of his face in a motorcycle crash. A Chunky Soup sponsorship also oversaw the rapid decline of once-elite running back LaDainian Tomlinson, forever casting into doubt the healthy properties of lean meat protein. Chunky Soup ads are also to blame for bringing Donovan McNabb's mother into national prominence, which isn't so much a jinx as a pox on all of us. Also, McNabb lost a Super Bowl in which he famously puked at the end. I bet if you analyzed that vomit that . . . yup, Chunky.

The Stetson Curse

There's only been one victim so far to fall prey to the Stetson Curse, but that victim was Tom Brady. Impressive, no? Brady first appeared in ads for the cologne in the fall of 2007. What happened? He went on to spoil a perfect season by losing Super Bowl XLII, only to have his ACL torn to ribbons the opening week of the following season. You might argue that one injury does not a curse make, but I'll argue that anything that helps bring down Tom Brady is worthy of inclusion on a list of curses. Or even getting its own wing in Canton.

V.4 Tailgating Is the Pregame Alcohol-Based Ritual of Kings

Ah, the tailgate. A bacchanalia of brews and brats that forms one of the most enjoyable aspects of the gameday experience, so naturally the NFL is doing everything within its power to stamp it out cold. It's not so much the gathering in the parking lot wearing team apparel part that league officials object to so much as the more central tailgating practice of eating your weight in Polish sausage and drinking yourself blind well before kickoff. That cuts into concession sales and makes for liability issues when people's cars get torched from parking over hot coals.

The modern incarnation of tailgating forms a convivial tableau, where thousands of people convene in a multitude of intermingling picniclike environments around their cars to eat, drink, socialize, toss the ball around, drink more, talk shit to fans of the opposing team, drink, smoke, play flipcup, drink while watching other people play flipcup, get asked to play cornhole, wonder aloud what cornhole is, give cornhole a shot and decide you kind of like it but could do without it, warble through team anthems, stand in line to piss for what seems like forever, drink while staring blankly at the asphalt, take a Jell-O shot, puke and rally, make out with random strangers, drink, and pass out. It's basically college in a parking lot.

There are forces that want to rob fans of the debauched pregame antics they automatically associate with a day of football. Indeed, the insidious fan conduct policy implemented in 2008 doesn't merely cover in-stadium behavior, but encompasses the parking lot surrounding the stadium. It may be nearly impossible to enforce in all cases, but it gives security officials free rein to get up in your business and ruin the fun. In that way, it's very similar to the Patriot Act, only possibly even more vaguely worded and invasive.

There are more distressing signs in the war on tailgating. Parking fees continue to climb, and while stadia increase in seating capacity, their parking lot sizes remain static, forcing tailgates into cheek by jowl positioning. In 2007, the company that owns a parking lot Seahawks fans had dubbed Hawk Heaven turned away tailgaters for a week. When an outcry by fans ensued, the company reversed its position, saying it would allow tailgaters, but no alcohol consumption, which is sort of like allowing Christmas without the rampant commercialism.

Tailgating was banned outside Super Bowl XLI in Miami, with officials citing suspect security reasons, and the policy was extended the following year at Super Bowl XLII in Arizona. It's a ridiculous about-face, of course, but one that rings all too familiar in the Roger Goodell era. Why has the NFL turned on something that has always been an integral part of its lifeblood? In the hopes of appearing palatable to some rare, possibly nonexistent breed of football fan that hates cursing, doesn't drink, abhors violence, and wants to worship at the puritanical altar of The Game as if it were a sort of state-run religion. I'm sure Kurt Warner loves that new direction. The rest of us just want to get sloppy and have a good time.

V.4.A AVOID TAILGATING SCENESTERS

Tailgating, as activities that involve alcohol usually do, has transformed into something of a subculture. There are those who travel the country only to experience the different tailgate scenes at any number of NFL and college football stadia or NASCAR tracks. Certainly these people cannot be blamed for embracing the boozier aspects of the fan experience, but many of them don't attend the events

these tailgates surround and have no interest in their out-
comes. Which is bizarre and borderline parasitic.

Beware these tailgating scenesters. Though they attempt to earn your trust with an array of interesting recipes
and odd novelty gadgets that have no application outside
a tailgate, they are roving partiers and nothing more. Instead of talking about the game, arguing about the game,
or even letting you know what kind of vested fantasy interests they have in the players involved, they want to gush
about how tailgating is the last great bastion of community
or some such nonsense. And that shit sucks out loud. If you
want a false sense of togetherness with your intoxication,
go to goddamn Burning Man.

A man named Joe Cahn has garnered national attention
for claiming the mantle of the Commissioner of Tailgating,
which is a bit like bearing the title Picnicmaster General.
Cahn, who maintains a Web site that promotes tailgating
culture and claims to be the world's only professional tail-
gater, has visited hundreds of stadia and sports complexes
and partied with thousands of revelers. While tailgating
is a fine slice of Americana and we're glad someone is out
there documenting its regional variations with the painstaking diligence of an ethnomusicologist, we generally
want to be around people who are into the game. Granted
foodies and lushes can come in handy by improving the
quality of the meats and liquor you stuff your face with,
but the last thing anyone wants is some windbag blubbering about the sense of kinship he feels with his common

man while you're trying to make a critical beer pong shot. Don't get all whimsical on me while I'm trying to get a buzz going.

V.4.B TAILGATING GRUB: MEAT, MEAT, MORE MEAT, WASH DOWN WITH BEER, REPEAT WITH MEAT

Not ingesting your weight in nitrates at the tailgate? That's a monstrous failure on your part. And not the heart failure that you should be encouraging. The staple of any tailgate is the fatty amalgam of wings, sausage, bacon, brats, beef patties, and any other assorted heart-clogging chunks of fatty flesh. There are those who clamor for vegetarian alternatives at the tailgate. There's no need to impose tofu dogs on those who don't consume them, so bring and cook your own veggie shit on the grill. And when you're dealing in things like wings, the less cutesy you get, the better. The buffalo wing is always a standard. Supplementing it with some fancy-dancy garlic parmesan or spicy Asian wings is well and good for the sake of variety, but these should by no means supplant the buffalo ones.

Most any combination of tasty meats and boozy drinks will serve you well when pregaming, though the fan should be encouraging to dabble in some of the expert creations the wild minds of expert tailgating are apt to create. A recent runaway phenomenon in tailgating circles is a dish known as Bacon Explosion, which combines two pounds of bacon and two pounds of sausage into one delectable artery-exploding log. Get someone to whip this up for your crew and you'll be set for a day. Provided there's enough refreshment to keep you tanked from arrival to the stadium walk-up.

V.5 Get Pumped for Victory in the Game You're Not Playing

This is football. It's no time for easy listening. You can play it mellow when gorging through the tailgate in hour one, but as kickoff approaches, you've got to get ready to spit hot fire. That means no techno, screamo, emo, jazz, classical, calypso, world music, ska, house, reggae, reggaeton, backpacker rap, pop punk, indie rock, or any of the other twee shit you'll hear on a Sufjan Stevens or a Belle and Sebastian album.

It's time for some auditory abuse that will knock you on your ass and take an asparagus-scented piss in your face. Having listened to these tracks, you'll be ready to drop-kick an opposing linebacker 20 yards downfield.

Let's not confuse these with the raft of tracks that blare out of the stadium sound system. "Crazy Train" by Ozzy, AC/DC tracks, or "Rock and Roll Part Two": these are far too commonplace to make it to your unique motivational playlist. Can't have others horning in on that. You need to know that you're not getting fed the same call to arms as every other schlub out there. Yours is singularly vicious. So here goes.

"Ante Up," M.O.P.—Consider this a check of your pulse. Not moving after this song means rigor mortis has set in and you belong deep, deep underground. Necrophiles patrol tailgates just to see who isn't responding to this track.

"Enter Sandman," Metallica—A sports pregame standby, but a classic for a reason. Granted, Metallica has largely been a pailful of suck for the better part of fifteen years, but this one maintains its motivational oomph, meaning it'll make you take a long jump between rooftops.

"Self Defense," Dilated Peoples—A song with a refrain that goes "You wanna hit us? We can hit back" and lyrics that include the reminder that "the best offense is a good defense" is clearly of relevance to a football crowd, even if what they're hitting each other with are gusts of flatus.

"What's My Name," DMX—Fiery and profane, and hence everything a fan can want in a song. What's more, Russell Simmons's doglike growls will make you feel like you're coming out of the tunnel with Joey Porter's pit bulls.

"Rise Above," Black Flag—Appropriating the fury of a song aimed at the conformist elements of society and then channeling it into emotional energy for a sports contest is what fans do best. Who cares what message anyone is trying to send out? The emotion is the point. And all the angry lyrics can be made to fit in a football context with enough booze.

"Protect Ya Neck," Wu-Tang Clan—More a helpful suggestion than a motivational tune. Maybe you can wear a Bryan Cox–like stiff neck collar under your uniform.

"Above the Clouds," Gang Starr—Among the pulsating tracks of venom, something a little more contemplative is in order. Lest you think that will make you go soft, Inspectah Deck's verse coupled with the Asiatic beats will make you want to lop enemy appendages off with Hitori Hanzo steel.

The last minute of Radiohead's "Electioneering" and the last two minutes of Guns N' Roses' "Paradise City"—Otherwise calm songs erupt in cacophonous mania, which is a perfect soundtrack to the anarchy you want to spill out into your gameday experience. These are great stretches of music to swing an unearthed security bollard to.

"Bodies," Drowning Pool—Are you a meathead in search of lifeless corpses falling to the ground with a thudding intensity? Then this might be just the kind of barking metal song you're looking for. Don't worry if you don't know any of the lyrics beyond "LET THE BODIES HIT THE FLO'!!" No one else does either.

"Lose Yourself," Eminem—Positively ubiquitous in the first few months following its release in 2002, this throbbing army march is enough to make you believe you're a desperate, destitute man fighting for his life, rather than a guy dropping thousands of dollars on season tickets.

"Play," David Banner—Not much point in an event teeming with pleas for ritualistic violence without a celebration of violent sexual encounters. If nearby women object, swear that the line "catch it in your mouth like your last name Moss" made you believe the song was about football.

"Bombs over Baghdad," Outkast—Because it's a catchy, energetic Outkast song that isn't "Hey Ya!" That alone will suffice.

"The Champ," Ghostface Killah—Clever lyricism is never more palatable to the football fan (especially the white one) than when it's packaged in a swaggering paean to kicking ass.

"Guerilla Radio," Rage Against the Machine—Need that final rush to get you ready to charge into the stadium and take the concession guy by the balls? Look no further. The final part of the song begins with a whispery Zack de la Rocha intoning, "It has to start somewhere. It has to start sometime. What better place than here? What better time than now?" Fuck and yes.

V.6 The High Five Is an Intricate Art Not to Be Toyed With

The purest expression of football fan exultation, save perhaps a belligerent flipping of the bird to an opposing fan, is the high five. It is a maneuver steeped in tradition, reeking of valor, and one that should not be overused or executed improperly. For any gesture so laden with import, some simple guidelines must be adhered to at all times. It may seem like a casual thing, this smacking of palms, but violate one of the hard-and-fast rules and the consequences could be dire.

Timing, as is often the case, is everything. Note that acceptable high-five-able scenarios are as follows:

- When your favorite team scores a touchdown or gets a pivotal third-down stop.
- When a fellow fan recounts how he hooked up with a girl from the bar (bonus five if she roots for your team).
- When someone on your fantasy team gets a big gain or a score and another person nearby is also starting that player. (Presumably you've let everyone within earshot know which players you're starting in any given week.) The five is rescinded if that player is going against your favorite team. Why are you starting him, anyway?
- Field goals and sacks, while not always sufficient to produce a high five, can be determined acceptable on a case-by-case basis. A game-winning field goal? Go for it. Settling for a field goal when down by two touchdowns? Not so much.
- When fiving in a bar or stadium, engaging in one five necessitates that you do the same for all adjacent fans of your team. It's like a toast in that sense. Leaving someone hanging is extremely poor form and will

likely leave you subject to a similar snubbing following the next score. Given the sensitivity of Seahawks fans, this might draw tears.

- An opposing fan may be issued a five if it is done as a means of distraction while a fellow fan ties his shoes together or steals his wallet.

The Classic

Room for variation exists within the high-five family, but tread carefully. The Classic involves throwing your arm forward at a near forty-five-degree angle with the palm facing forward. This is the vintage, more exuberant *high* five. A bit campy, but undeniably infectious. The Variation is the more greeting-friendly *regular* five, which involves one person, the fivee, placing his palm supine and the other, the fiver, slapping his palm downward onto the waiting hand of the fivee. This is the more informal maneuver, and its distinction from the high five mirrors the difference between a hug and a handshake. Except fans are judged more harshly for their fives than regular folk are for their handshakes. Firm handshake but awkward five? Very questionable.

You must actually make full contact with your co-fiver's hand. You wouldn't believe how many people botch this one. A glancing blow off the other person's hand is just as awkward as a full miss. Like horseshoes, hand grenades, and hand jobs, there is no almost in high fives. And alcohol is no excuse for failed hand-eye coordination. The government would be well advised to add a high-five exam on the driving test. Young, drunk, and face-palmed is no way to go through life.

This is about as extravagant as you can get if you're a white guy. Black people may press the flesh further. White guys, you may observe them in awe, but by no means should you attempt to imitate them. They know what they're doing. You do not.

The Fist Bump and Fist Pound

The fist bump and fist pound are slightly less orthodox, but perfectly acceptable substitutes for the high five. However, they should be used only in conjunction with the high five, in the way ranch dip is used to complement wings. A person who employs the fist bump alone is not only limiting himself as a fan, but possibly stepping into danger's path by constantly proffering his fist in strangers' faces. When those people are drunk, the potential for trouble reaches Pacman-in-Vegas levels.

The Chest Bump and Ass Bump

The chest bump and the more dreaded ass bump should only be executed with a strong sense of irony and ideally with someone of the opposite gender. Tailgating would be the best time to pull off such a move, if at all. Make sure everyone in the vicinity has tied a few on and is ready to laugh at wacky, borderline uncomfortable hijinks. With the mood is relaxed, you're less likely to have objects hurled your way. Remember, that's less likely, not entirely unlikely.

V.7 Like All Extreme Sports, Running onto the Playing Field Is Dumb and Wrong—and Irresistible

Sinister forces of temptation goad you toward the forbidden. Alcohol has done its part to convince you that it is doable. From your close-in seat in the fifth row, all that separates you from the stomping grounds of your beloved gladiators is a quick plunge over the wall and the swarming gauntlet of a couple dozen security guards and police officers. Nothing you can't handle. It's a scenario you've been turning over in your head for years, but you never thought you'd find yourself in a mindset to act on it. If you can just bob and weave enough, make a few guys miss, you can be on the field long enough to steal a cheerleader grope or maybe even slap the smug clear off Jack Del Rio's assface. After that, who knows, the means for a daring escape should present itself. You can think on your feet.

But, wait, you've seen this before. All those arm-flailing fucktards on *SportsCenter* reels and YouTube clips scurrying on the field for a few fleeting moments before getting ingloriously force-fed some turf by security. Nah. You're better than them. They looked so . . . so loutish. You're above all that, someone who can sprinkle Gallicisms in your inner monologues, far above such gutter exploits and . . . and you've already gone, haven't you? It sucks being a drunk person's conscience. Always being on a five-second delay, like a network television live broadcast. Instead of filtering out swearing, it keeps out reason.

Streaking is not advocated, mostly because you're almost certainly going to get gang tackled by mouth-breathing rent-a-cops, arrested, and banned from the stadium for life, in the process making a public jackass of yourself and your family.

Finding yourself unable to quell the demons that compel you to rush the field? At least try to keep them at bay until an opportune moment. Or get some cash out of the deal. At the very least, only make an attempt if you know you're slippery enough to evade capture for a solid minute or so. Nothing is quite as sad as someone who wastes his one big chance at public jackassery with the epic failure of immediate apprehension. If you do, despite all the logical reasons that say you shouldn't, decide to take a shot, here are some sound suggestions:

Get an unscrupulous company to sponsor you.— That's what serial streaker Mark Roberts did when he ran out onto the field during Super Bowl XXXVIII. Hopping a knee-high barrier at Reliant Stadium, he stripped down to a G-string and shoes with a plug for gambling site GoldenPalace.com scrawled on his chest. For this, he got slapped with a $1,000 fine yet avoided any jail time. And that was during the motherfucking Super Bowl. That's like calling in a bomb threat to the White House and getting a point on your driver's license. The terms of the sponsorship were never disclosed, but even if it was a financial wash, he got to streak during the Super Bowl with little or no consequence. That's more than a little awesome.

If you're going naked, be sure to wave your junk at the opposing team.—It'll not only assert dominance, but remind them of the days when Charles Haley was in the league.

If you're a woman and going naked, be sure to wave your junk at the camera.—It's just common courtesy. Unless you're a Packers fan. Then please disregard. And put on four more layers.

Have a sympathetic angle ready.—In 2005, a forty-four-year-old man ran onto the field in Philadelphia holding a plastic bag emitting a cloud of dust from his outstretched arm before dropping to his knees on the 30-yard line and making the sign of the cross. Was he trying to be the next Johnny Anthraxseed? Nope. Turns out he was spreading the ashes of his recently deceased mother, who was an avid Eagles fan. Sure, it didn't stop kneejerk security storm troopers from detaining him, but you bet your beer-battered ass it inspired some clemency.

Remember that the players have bottled-up fan animosity.—It can't be stressed too much that the yellow-jacketed Gestapo are not your only obstacles during your jaunts onto the playing field. The players themselves will be all too happy to assist in your undoing. It's not that they're upset to have a stoppage in play. Most of them are probably exhausted and glad to have the brief respite. However, after years of having to hold back from lashing out at fans in the face of intense personal criticism on things beyond viewers' comprehension, the chance to clothesline a fan with impunity is an opportunity a player cannot soon pass up. So resist the urge to pat a linebacker on the shoulder lest you feel like getting speared in the ribs.

Disrupt the game (but only if it helps your team).— In October 2005, a fan in Cincinnati rushed the field in the final minute of a Bengals-Packers game, snatching the ball from then-Packers QB Brett Favre and causing the play to be blown dead. At the time, the Packers were trailing 21-14 and trying to drive for a tying score, with the ball inside Bengals' territory. The five-minute break the incident caused allowed the Bengals' winded defense to regroup. Favre was then sacked on the following play, which contributed heavily to sealing the win for Cincy. As you can see, it's the opportunistic and savvy disruptive fan who wins the day. That he ends up getting buried alive hours later by guys who put money on the game is another matter entirely.

V.8 The Challenge of the Superfans

In the annals of rabid fandom, only a privileged few have reached the lofty heights of the superfan, where the standard-issue fanatic transcends the mundane acts of regular cheering and becomes something more. The superfan can come off as a deranged soul possessed with the flair of a Broadway costume designer. To those who know better, they are lovably intense folks you're happy to have on your side. Superfans are held in such esteem among those in their own fan base that they, in effect, become synonymous with the franchise itself. Granted, the privilege of being one earns a whole lot of bubkes. In fact, the effort necessary to be recognized as a superfan will set you back a pretty penny, nevertheless you'll be paid back tenfold with the admiration of hordes of drunk people.

No sporting league honors its most frighteningly faithful quite like the NFL. From 1999 to 2005, Visa sponsored a special display at the Pro Football Hall of Fame called the Hall of Fans. Each year during that span, one fan representing each team was chosen to be added to this pantheon of pathology. After Visa ended its sponsorship, the selection process was shelved, but the display remains. Presumably next to the exhibit of photographs of owners bathing in money reaped from charging outrageous amounts for personal seat licenses.

It's just as well that the annual inductions ended. Most teams are fortunate if they have one iconic fan, let alone six or more. Hell, the Cardinals organization is thrilled if their stadium is less than 60 percent road fans. Also, letting in thirty-some-odd candidates a year dilutes the honor considerably. If anything, it should be conducted like the selection process for the regular Hall of Fame, where there are at most a handful of entrants each year and they are voted on by putatively objective writers who let petty grudges and arbitrary factors decide who should and shouldn't get in. That seems to work okay.

Superfan status can't be attained overnight. It takes years of painstaking gimmick-honing and camera-mugging. There's no hope for cheapskates, either. You have to be front and center for the networks to pick you up on crowd shots. Every game too. That means season tickets in the front row, no less. Simply follow the example of these fans who have carved out a place for themselves in football fandom lore.

Chief Zee—Zema Williams, a fixture at Redskins games for more than three decades, wears a full head-dress and carries a twelve-inch tomahawk with him to games at the unbearable FedEx Field. He's earned his war paint too. In a 1983 visit to Veterans Stadium in Philly, Chief Zee had his leg broken and his costume torn by murderous Eagles fans. And yet, he was not pelted with a single battery. I'd say he got off easy by Eagles fan standards. The Redskins, of course, can also boast the rooting presence of a troop of twelve cross-dressing pig fans known as the Hogettes. But they don't appear in Eastern Motors commercials.

Fireman Ed—Ed Anzalone is believed by some to be the originator of the Jets' signature "J-E-T-S, JETS, JETS, JETS" chant. This immediately negates any heroism cred he may have accumulated as a member of the New York City fire department.

Catman—The six-four, 340-pound Greg Good attends every home game at Bank of America Stadium sporting a giant blue shock of hair, a cape, and two oversized blue Incredible Hulk–sized fists. Now, when you refer to the Panthers colors, you have to say Carolina blue, because the state is annoying enough to try to lay claim to a shade of a color.

Birdman—Not to be confused with Harvey Birdman, Joseph Ripley sticks with the obvious animal theme in his fandom foolery, much like NFC rival Catman. Birdman wears a beak underneath his face mask-less helmet, along with a rather aerodynamic cape. Using his power of flight, he can change up the usual Eagles fan approach by dropping nine volts on you from above.

Barrel Man—Proof positive that your superfan gimmick need not have anything to do with the team name itself, Tim McKernan spent thirty years in the service for his beloved Broncos, looking like a hobo in the stands at Mile High Stadium and even getting a Super Bowl ring from the team in 1998. In 2007, he finally hung up his barrel. Hopefully he had something on underneath.

The Packalope—A play on the mystical jackalope, a cross between a jackrabbit and an antelope, the Packalope, Larry Primeau, wears a throwback Packers helmet with a ten-point deer rack attached. Citing a new policy on banned weapons, Lambeau Field officials have prohibited Primeau from wearing his antlers inside the stadium. Yet the foam Cheeseheads remain. Their ability to poke your eyes out may not be as strong, but they are the key obstacle in the war against tacky.

Mr. and Mrs. Seahawk—Notable wigged spousal members of the 12th Man, which is the oh-so-novel name the Seahawks fan base attaches to itself. Indeed, the happy couple was instrumental in helping to steal the name from Texas A&M.

Bill Swerski—Sticklers for facts will point out that Swerski and his band of Bears superfans are not, in fact, real, but since when does reality have anything to do with football fandom? The *Saturday Night Live* caricature of sports fanaticism has done more to shape the archetype of crazed fan behavior than booze and bachelorhood combined.

The Bone Lady—While there are any number of recognizable fans in Cleveland's infamous Dawg Pound, including Big Dawg and Dawg Pound Mike, none of them are as chesty as the Bone Lady. Debra Darnell transforms herself into this near-superhuman figure for Browns games, replete with accessory laden beehive and cat glasses. The Bone Lady rides around in her tricked-out Bone Mobile, a Volvo station wagon that she has suffused in team memorabilia and to the roof of which she has added an eight-foot lighted bone. Quite an effort for an obvious double entendre.

Dolfan Denny—Denny Sym began leading Miami crowds in cheers during the Dolphins' first game in 1966. Ten years later, the owner asked him to become the team's official motivator for fifty dollars a game. You know it was a magical time, because that might have actually covered the cost of the ticket he bought to get in. Sym died in March 2007.

Crazy Ray—Wilford Jones's charming antics—along with his signature chaps, six-shooter, and blue vest—almost made you forget that Cowboys fans are by and large insufferable fuckwits. The sports world lost him a day after Dolfan Denny passed away.

Boltman—Originally hired by the Chargers in 1995 as a mascot, the costumed character later broke with the team to do his own thing. Boltman wears a Chargers uniform over a muscle suit with an almost crescent-shaped bolt head and sunglasses, causing him to bear an amazing resemblance to '80s McDonald's pitch-moon Mac Tonight.

Arrowman—Among a crowd of self-decribed su-perfans in Kansas City that includes First Down Elvis, Red Xtreme, Weirdwolf, XFactor, and Retro Fan, Ar-rowman dons a jersey and hat of the Chiefs' opponent with an array of gag arrows shot through his head and torso. Because there's no better way to stick it to another team than buying up their merchandise.

100 Percent Cheese-Free—A friend to vegans and Packers haters everywhere, Sid Davy is a Vikings fan who lives in Winnipeg and commutes seven hours to each game at the Metrodome, where he dons a cos-tume similar to a Norse version of Hulk Hogan, with purple face paint, chain mail, a Viking helmet, and long, blond ponytails. True to his hulkish image, his biceps rival even those of Ed Hochuli, though he has a ways to go before he rivals Hochuli's ability to blow plays dead prematurely. In 2008, Davy ventured all the way to Massachusetts to attend a Patriots-Broncos game so that he could reunite with his favorite player, Randy Moss, who was fond of jumping into Cheese-Free's massive arms in the first row of the stands during his days in Minnesota. This despite the fact that Moss stopped playing for the Vikes four years earlier.

Darth Raider—A fixture of the Black Hole in Oakland who wears a Darth Vader mask and some Legion of Doom–esque spiked shoulder pads. Really frightening until you realize it's Hayden Christensen under the mask.

Fan Man—One of those Ravens fans who adores purple camouflage pants, this one at least has the benefit of legacy on his side. Matt Andrews is the nephew of the best-known Baltimore Colts fan, "Willie the Rooter." He converted a 1986 Astro van into the Fan Van by painting it purple, adding Ravens decals, and getting players and coaches to sign it at training camp. Knowing Baltimore, it's held more than a few dead bodies in the back.

V.9 Gamble, Because of Course You're Smarter than Vegas

You don't need me to tell you that gambling is the refuge of filthy degenerates, which explains why reasonable football fans gravitate to it so eagerly. Just as fantasy football heightens the importance of individual achievement, gambling ratchets up the significance of team effort, whether that be losing by no more than six points or helping to push the point total of the game above 42, thereby earning you a cool three grand and the chance to see your daughter again.

The NFL maintains an uneasy relationship with gambling. Seemingly every mainstream publication that covers the league prints the lines that Vegas gives on the games each week, as well as providing picks based on those spreads, yet includes the disclaimer that such odds are for recreational purposes only. Which is kind of like when Hollywood puts Jessica Alba in a movie and expects me not to jerk it in the theater. Why the hell else would I be there?

The government is no more receptive toward our yearning to worship at the altar of Gamblor, the six-penised polytheistic deity of wagering. Big Government makes it its business to quash every sports gambling opportunity that exists outside of Vegas, just because it's a haven for organized crime, though certainly less of one than the underground structures that form in lieu of a legal betting system. Besides, hating the mafia is sheer lunacy, because there's nothing Americans love more than organized crime, especially when its depicted in movies and

TV shows. Just take the word of 49ers fans, all of whom would give their left one to get Eddie DeBartolo and the mob back in the front office.

By falling back on shoddy appeals to morality, the government's stance on gambling makes as much sense as its war on drugs. It's been estimated that the underground sports betting market in the United States hovers around $150 billion. Think of all that potential revenue squandered. It's enough to turn people into libertarians, but then they'd have to agree with insufferably smug Bill Maher.

In fact, Montana, hardly a state known for its tilt toward innovation, has recently instituted an NFL-based fantasy football lottery game. Granted, along with Delaware, Nevada, and Oregon, it's one of the four states where sports betting is legal, but this is still a daring step in the right direction. Naturally, the lottery game isn't approved by the NFL, which should signal all the more that it's something people will enjoy. Until legislators come to their senses (which is usually right around the time it becomes politically expedient to do so) football fans will be forced to keep alive hope that their credit card doesn't get rejected by Bodog. The Nanny State and the NFL may tut-tut its existence, but people are going to find ways to gamble, like it or lump it. As for strategies, I'm no Brandon Lang. I don't have the secrets to gambling success, other than that you should always bet against whichever team starts Rex Grossman at QB or has Marvin Lewis patrolling the sidelines. Also, stay away from road favorites in the playoffs. And I'm pretty sure wagering big on your favorite team is a money pit from which you'll never escape. That said, sweeping secrets to gambling success are hard to come by, unless you pull a Biff from *Back to the Future* and swipe a sports almanac from a far-off year. The one nugget of advice is, don't think you're smarter than Vegas. Down this road of thought lies financial rack and ruin. If a spread looks ridiculous, it's that way for a reason. After all, Vegas was built on compulsive types who thought they were smarter than Vegas. People like Charles Barkley.

V.10 Probably Should've Known Before You Bought Those Season Tickets: Watching a Game at Home Is Far Better than the Stadium Experience

For better or worse, we've entered a golden age for the couch potato. Gyrate your flabby appendages in celebration and count your blessings, if not the calories. Just as advances in home video technology have ruined much of the draw of heading to the multiplex, so too has the great leap forward in the fan experience for the homebody been brought about by the rise of the Internet and improvements to television broadcast production, which has coincided with how NFL owners have done everything in their power to ruin the live experience.

While seeing the game in a stadium packed to the gills with rabid fans is the purest and most glorious experience in fanhood, one must be prepared to stare down hours of traffic, fight with drunken assholes, pay impossibly high ticket and concession prices, accept poor sight lines, and endure Russian-breadline-like queues to the bathroom. And that's before you get ejected because someone squealed on you to security for offending them by yelling that T.J. Houshmandzadeh is a rat-tailed queef goddess.

The dirty secret of fandom is that going to an NFL game can really suck ass sometimes, at least compared with the experience of watching from the comfort of your home or a good sports bar. It seems counterintuitive to those raised believing a seat in the stands beats a seat on the couch, but it's true. And it's doubly so if you're a fan of a team that has decided to dump their stadium out in the middle of an inaccessible sprawly suburban hellhole or in New Jersey.

The advent of HDTV and satellite programming packages has made the difference all the more pronounced. What you see on your flat screen looks as good, if not better, than what your view would be from a $150 seat in the 500 Level, though seeing ESPN NFL reporter John Clayton in high definition has been known to result in irreparable orbital occlusion. Still, the advantages to home viewing are innumerable. At home, you can gorge on the finest in meats, libations, and Cheez Doodles without an inflated price or fourth-quarter liquor cutoff rules. You can make it to the bathroom during timeouts. You can totally whip it out and jerk it to cheerleaders without being arrested. It's great.

One hitch in the deal is enduring the platitudinal ramblings of play-by-play announcers. Oh, Eli Manning is actually an ice water–veined field general, is he, Dierdorf? Mike Tomlin's bravado just oozes out of him, does it?

Philip Rivers hasn't thrown a misplaced floating pass in his life? Die. They're enough to make you jab stretched out paper clips into your eardrums. There are a number of potential solutions for negating their brain cramping prowess. For a local game, there's the popular option of muting the TV while listening to the game commentary on the radio. Or one can ignore commentators altogether and watch the game while blasting your favorite music. Unless the dulcet tones of Cris Collinsworth's nasally breakdown of a quarterback hitting the checkdown receiver is like birdsong to your tin ears, in which case you're already fanatically bankrupt.

That isn't to say the live experience doesn't still hold appeal. Certainly nothing at home or at a bar can touch the palpable energy of a packed stadium during a tight game. We as fans would prefer the live experience to the televised one, but given how it's priced beyond our means and that our behavior is being restricted more and more every year, it's becoming increasingly difficult to muster the will to get out to the stadium. At this point, being able to tell people you attended an event is, for many, is about as important as how much fun you have while you're there. For the league, or any entertainer, the benefit of exploiting that basic human need for anecdotes to share with others cannot be understated.

Purists will wheeze the claim that television's rise has always come at the expense of the live game. Not that there's no truth to that. In person, TV timeouts are a frequent but jarring break in the action, in which any fluid pacing of the game is broken up. Meanwhile, the timeouts encompass too little time to do anything but make small talk with the person next to you in the lovingly constructed full-body bird costume.

Before proponents of other sports start getting all fussy, affirming that this proves the NFL is nothing more than an overblown, plodding spectacle, know that this argument is just as true for their, ahem, games as it is for The One True Sport. With the exception of baseball, of course, which is actually better to watch in person than on television, but that's only by virtue of baseball being so excruciating to watch on TV. Stupid languid baseball broadcast camera. I need frantic cutting and animated dancing robots, not one camera angle from center field. When will you learn?

Owners aren't idiots, of course. All right, Mike Brown is. Some of them may not be able to run a winning franchise, but the policies they set as a collective tend to work out well for them in terms of the whole making-money-hand-over-fist thing. They wouldn't have spent decades bleeding you dry if they weren't good at it, willing though you may be to let them.

Will there ever be a breaking point? Many franchises, even as they hike prices and restrict what you can do, have waiting lists for season tickets measured in years, if not decades. Should the televised experience supplant the live one as the viewing experience of choice for fans, won't that only serve to increase the number of commercial interruptions? Possibly. But then, I envision a breaking point when fans head to luxury boxes with sharp sticks and torches. After that, everything should be alllllll right.

ARTICLE VI

The Fantasy Football Chapter (Now with Tear-Out Cheat Sheet!)

VI.1 Fantasy Baseball Is for Geeks but Fantasy Football Is for Men

In just the span of the last decade, fantasy football has gone from being the dominion of tens of millions socially backward statistics-fixated sports-enthused geeks to a widely celebrated veritable superorgy of man-children.

Because only football is badassed enough to make a geeky pursuit like rotisserie leagues a phenomenon that has become even quasi-acceptable in mainstream male culture. According to the Fantasy Sports Trade Association, more than 80 percent of people who played any fantasy sport played fantasy football. Naturally, they could have played in other sport leagues as well, but, uh, RAWR, FOOTBALL!

In many ways, fantasy has come to shape the rudiments of football fandom and challenge some of our most basic assumptions about rooting interests. Though no real fan would ever wish for a fantasy football victory if it comes at the expense of a defeat to his real-life team.

But what if it's Week 13 and your real-life team is impossibly out of playoff contention and, if the superstar receiver of the team you're playing that week can just get a touchdown and at least 70 yards, you'll win the money league for the first time ever? Sorry, still got to support the team. Fantasy football, by its very nature, invites you to consider rival players as individuals, as people. And that can simply not be. Rivals are not to be empathized with. That you even have rival players on your fantasy team is a horrible slight to your fellow members of [*insert team name*] Nation.

Your real life team always takes primacy in all non-gambling matters. It should be noted that there is a small but critical difference between gambling against your team and rooting against them with fantasy in mind. In gambling against your team, you're finding a clever way to recoup money in exchange for your suffering. If it's a big game, you may do it to protect against the huge kick in the nuts that will result if your team loses. It's a small consolation you'll be glad to forfeit if it means you're jinxing the other team.

It's astounding how much fantasy has permeated the entire football experience. Some players in the NFL admit to playing in fantasy leagues. Hot-pants-wearing Redskins tight end Chris Cooley dolefully reported that his three-touchdown performance in a game in December 2005 caused one of his four fantasy teams to be eliminated from playoff contention because his opponent had started Cooley.

Believe it or not, but fantasy football was the first good thing ever to come out of Oakland. Had to be something. In 1962, Raiders co-owner Bill Winkenbach, Raiders PR employee Bill Tunnell, *Oakland Tribune* sportswriter Scotty Sterling, and editor George Ross, trying to entertain themselves during a three-week road trip, formed the first fantasy league. Taking their cue from the long-established baseball rotisserie leagues. They named it the Greater Oakland Professional Pigskin Prognosticators League. Surely this occasion needs to be honored with some sort of federal holiday, preferably one in late August, so people can more easily brush off social and business obligations in favor of holding the draft. This needs to be a national priority.

The emergence of the Internet allowed it to take off, as football fans aren't so high on math, and having automated live scoring done by a computer helps take the time commitment issue out of it. That and it puts fantasy sports and porn in one handy little package. Thank you, magical Internet box.

Fantasy has become so huge that networks and august sports news publications have hired supposed experts for the sole purpose of discussing the fantasy implications of each NFL game. Of course, this has nothing to do with the studies that show that fantasy players on average buy more tickets to sporting events and spend more money at stadia than do other sports fans.

And why not? Fantasy improves all facets of football. A December game between the Texans and the Rams is an otherwise unwatchable affair between two clubs playing for draft picks. The players don't care. Even their fans don't care. No one cares. That is unless the game has fantasy implications for you. If so, you'll be spending the entire game in rapt attention, you'll formulate at least thirty game scenarios that result in Andre Johnson getting the 21 points you need. Of course, you'll find your head in an oven when he only delivers 20, after he fumbles the ball on his final garbage-time catch with the team already up three scores.

The popularity does not dilute the passion that most bring to fantasy football. In fact, all signs indicate the first fantasy-related homicide is near. Last year, a thirty-eight-year-old Florida man held a knife to his roommate's neck and threatened to kill him in a dispute that began over fantasy scoring. Alarmists will decry this, but fantasy-related violence is typically relegated to imagined scenarios where fantasy players exact ghastly revenge against NFL players who performed well during weeks they were benched by their fantasy owners.

VI.2 Know Your Fantasy League or Know Draft Defeat

When diving headlong into the choppy waters of fantasy football, it helps to know that the act of drafting is an intricate science. Sure, for the uncommitted, there's always the option of auto-drafting to your heart's content and getting whacked on a weekly basis by every other owner in the league. Whatever works for you. Those who are ready to sack up do their homework. Every league wants a couple patsies to pony up entry money they have no chance of winning back.

Before even deciding on which format to enter into, you should know there's no reason to ever get involved with a public league (unless it carries a mammoth prize, but even then you should supplement it with private leagues). What's the point of fantasy triumph if it's not something you can lord over someone you know? Someone like a friend or a coworker who has no choice but to absorb your vicious taunts with quiet resentment. You simply can't get that satisfaction in a public league. And make a point not to sign up for any league that doesn't offer head-to-head contests. League-wide rotisserie formats are the worst idea a group of people has entered into aside from cuddle parties. Even survivor leagues, where a team need only not be the lowest scoring team in its league to advance from week to week, don't provide a sufficient rush. Fantasy football isn't a war of attrition. It's supposed to mirror the NFL itself by being a series of bitter duels to determine who gets to advance to meaningful bitter duels.

The type of league you join will dictate which type of draft you go through. It's not only the draft that your choice affects; it has other long-term consequences as well, forcing you to select players with an eye toward more than just the immediate future. Matt Millen hates those.

There are generally two types of drafts: the normal kind and the incredibly involved kind that makes you focus on numbers and hurts your thinkin' box in ways that have nothing to do with polluting it with booze.

> **Standard Draft**—The bog standard model, in which you're free to take whoever you'd like in serpentine order without regard to performance beyond the season or how the players' predetermined value factors into your budget. For most casual player, this is the tits.
>
> **Auction Draft**—But nooooo, there are people who want to make their hobbies as close to having a second job as a GM as humanly possible. In these leagues, dollar amounts are assigned to players as though they were free agents on an imaginary market. You, as a fantasy owner, have to work each draftee into your budget. This concept is usually extended into salary-cap leagues, where the budget must be considered when making trades and acquiring free agents throughout the season. Again, it's possible—there's a faint chance—that you're making too much work for yourself.
>
> **Standard League**—Again, no fuss, no muss. You have the players you drafted, but you can sign or trade for new players solely based on availability and the willingness of your trade partner (or how well you

can steal their passwords and furtively force them to accept a trade).

Dynasty Leagues—In a Dynasty League, fantasy owners retain the players they draft from one season to the next, with rookies being the only players drafted with each successive season. So one regrettable draft has the potential to ream you for multiple years instead of mere months. Sounds like a blast.

Keeper Leagues—The keeper league operates in much the same manner as a dynasty league, in that players can be retained by the same owner from one season to the next, though it's typically only a handful as opposed to the entire roster, thus giving owners a better chance for unfucking themselves following poor drafts and critical injuries the year previous.

IDP Leagues—For the hard-core fan who can appreciate some defense, IDP leagues are marked by the drafting of individual defensive players in lieu of the entire defense as a unit, which is the norm in most fantasy leagues.

Malfeasance Leagues—In general, fantasy football focuses on the positive, though there are so many delectably horrible things in the NFL to celebrate. With the malfeasance league, you can make disgraceful behavior work for you. This league awards points for arrests (one for DUI, two for drug possession, three for drug distribution, four for domestic violence, five for random aggravated assault, six for murder, seven for deviant sexual acts, etc.) as well as for suspensions and being a clubhouse cancer. Did a player on your team just throw a teammate under the bus to the press? Score a point for you. Until you signed up, you couldn't stand dirty players like Albert Haynesworth or bad apples like Matt Jones. Now they're the best contributors to your lineup.

Okay, okay, this last type of league doesn't technically exist, but it needs to happen. Enterprising fans of the world, let's do this. For the betterment of fankind.

Once settled on a league, the first concern of a draftee is the structure of the team being put together. How many receivers, running backs, and flex players (a slot on the lineup open to either a back, a receiver, or a tight end) are set in your lineup? Next, you have to know the scoring value assigned to each statistic. Are you in a points-per-reception league? If so, are you content salivating over underneath-route-dwelling receivers like Wes Welker? Does the league give points for return yardage on special teams? It does? What kind of bullshit league did you join? How many do you get per passing touchdown? How many yards does your quarterback have to throw for you to get a point? Arcane though they may seem, the answers to these questions will go a long way toward determining your drafting board and ultimately the gang of disappointments whose names you will curse until the end of days, or at least the end of the season.

The league commissioner will ultimately make these calls. The job of commissioner is a thankless one in which the poor sap thrust into the role will have to preside over petty complaints of unfair trades, deal with people who are slow to pay their membership fees, and perform the rest of the administrative duties only a type A personality could derive pleasure from. But with great responsibility comes, well, not a whole lot of power. You could abuse your authority to change league rules in your favor, but there's also nothing to stop your league mates from beating you with socks filled with nickels if you do.

VI.3 Naming Your Fantasy Team, or Which Anchorman Reference Shall You Go With?

The naming of your fantasy team is an act of equal, possibly even greater importance than naming your children, and deserves at least as much thought and intoxication to nail down. This may come as a painful realization, but almost certainly your team isn't going to triumph in its league. In addition to loss of pride and countless hours of work, you will also forfeit whatever money you paid to enter your league. You should be prepared for this.

In the face of such excruciating failure, your only hope for saving face, besides blaming the randomness of injuries and shady waiver deals for ruining your otherwise fantastic drafting performance, is the genius of your team name.

There exists but one inviolable rule for fantasy team

naming: be funny. This is a tall task for any football fan because, on the whole, football fans are overly serious dipshits.

It's easy. Dick jokes, fart jokes, tit jokes, fat jokes, movie quotes, fantasy violence, violence, mockery of the poor, epithets both racial and religious, contempt for the wealthy, sexual deviancy, blind anger, focused anger, low-grade homophobia, mild cripplephobia, intense xenophobia, sexism, retards, and even SIDS can all be funny, given a deft enough touch.

If you happen to be in a league with work colleagues or women, you should probably knock that list down to movie quotes. Also, why the hell are you in a league with women?

Ultimately, the greatest challenge for any fantasy team name is braving the test of time. Most often, a name has enough humorous oomph to survive maybe a few weeks of laughs before becoming incredibly tiresome. You must strive for a name that can endure over the course of a season.

Chances are, that timeless resplendent gem of hilarity isn't going to come to you. That's fine. You're just a boring asshole is all. At the very least, you can try to be topical. Beware though. While it may be tempting to riff off the biggest story of the off-season, the key to being funny is being original. And deeply offensive. But mostly original.

For example, remember back in the beginning of the 2007 season after Michael Vick was sent to prison for running a dog-fighting ring? Sure, it was an endless source of laughs. However, every other doucheweasel had a fantasy team name playing on an aspect of that scandal. It was "rape stand" this and "Bad Newz Kennel Club" that. A month into the season and a Michael Vick joke was as tired as "I'm Rick James, bitch." Beware that trap by anticipating the longevity of a crude reference. Think long and hard before cursorily submitting Visante Shiancock for your fantasy team this year. Surely there was some obscure player who got in a hilarious drug bust during the off-season from which you can draw material. The police blotter is the stuff of which great fantasy names are made.

It should be noted that if you are playing in multiple leagues (and if you aren't, why not? Who are you, President Obama? Your time isn't that valuable) you may absolutely *not* recycle team names. Not from years past. Not from your teams in other leagues. It's out of the question.

VI.4 The Fantasy Draft Is the Only Time Being an Unrepentant Homer Doesn't Help

Here's when the whole of your strategic genius is brought to bear. Do you start going all homer and scoop up every player possible from your real-life favorite team? It bespeaks hard-core fandom, even if it's a sure-fire recipe for disaster in fantasy. Especially if your real-life team happens to the Lions or the Raiders. Conversely, do you eschew your favorite team entirely, fearing that your fanhood will blind you to players' actual worth, or worse still, that having them on your fantasy team will jinx members of the real-life team irreparably? Both approaches, it should be noted, are incredibly asinine.

Now where to convene to divvy up players like European monarchs divvied up Africa? Weighing the options for the location of your draft will at least enable you to make a mistake from an informed perspective.

THE BAR

Pro: Reduced chance of wife walking in mid-draft to tell you to watch the kids.

Con: People in public who aren't predisposed to understand your nerdish leanings judging you as the embarrassing tool you are.

SOMEONE'S HOUSE

Pro: Not having to pony up cash for every drink; chance to geek out without eliciting disdainful looks from attractive women, as there will be none present.

Con: The possibility of family members seeing you at your most man-childish.

INTERNET DRAFT FROM HOME

Pro: Can masturbate to your sexy draft class without objection, judgment, or arrest.

Con: The flow and spontaneity of trash-talk is ruined by slow typing.

COFFEE HOUSE

Pro: Caffeine is superior to booze as a drug for maintaining steely focus on your fantasy team.

Con: Paucity of far tastier booze, abundance of leering quasi-intellectuals who consider football fandom to be only marginally more respectable than pederasty.

SAUNA

Pro: No less homoerotic than a fantasy football draft in any other setting.

Con: Wi-Fi connection may be compromised by steam.

STRIP CLUB

Pro: A setting where you get expensively teased is appropriate for an activity in which you foolishly delude yourself into thinking you're an NFL general manager.

Con: A member of your league inevitably gets thrown out for hugging a dancer after somehow landing Thomas Jones in the third round.

VI.4.A DRAFT TRASH-TALK TIPS

- Laugh rapturously anytime someone selects a defense prior to the last round, no matter how much sense it makes.
- At least once per round, announce that a pick is a reach. If the person contests this claim, scream "rreeeeeeaaaaacccchhhhhh." And hit them.

- When it gets to the point that someone drafts Jake Delhomme, make a point of getting out of your seat and declaring the draft to be over. An exaggerated gesture, like throwing your draft board over your shoulder, punctuates this statement.
- If you're not stealing glances at others' draft boards, you're not trying.
- Defaming someone's mom is the best way to deal with another draftee taking a player you were looking to take with your next pick. Even if you are related to this person.
- If you draft Braylon Edwards, you might as well castrate yourself on the spot. Though you'll probably drop the knife.

VI.5 Fantasy Football Magazines Are the Most Useless Things You'll Reflexively Purchase Each Year

Without question, the fantasy football magazine is one of the most disappointing consumer items on the market, right up there with rechargeable batteries and the Sham-Wow. Yet there remain approximately eight thousand different kinds available for purchase, and not a useful one among them. Thing is, most fans don't want to commit the time needed to properly prepare for a draft. That's an act bordering on studying. The one thing more antisocial than pouring your free time into managing your fantasy team is pouring copious free time into getting ready to compile your fantasy team. It's like reading an anatomy book before going to Fuck Town. Sure, the detailed pictures are enticing, but it's so creepy that even Sean Salisbury would feel dirty doing it.

For the nine dollars you throw down for these prodigious wastes of ink, you're inundated with hundreds upon hundreds of bland player capsules and tedious team previews, none of which actually assist with fantasy drafting in the least. What's more, all of this information is easily accessible and, most importantly, free online. What it comes down to is that most of the buyers of these mags, lazy bastards though they are, pick them up only to remove the cheat sheet that lists the top 150 players and the best twenty at each position. Again, this is a commodity that can either be printed out in full or culled together using little effort via free resources on the Internet. And the resources online didn't have to go to print three months before the preseason starts, making their advice as potentially outdated as a Peter King iTunes recommendation.

The promise of identifying sleepers (players who have surprisingly productive or breakout years, better known as the guys you end up passing on in favor of Ronald Curry) is another hook that these publications use to bamboozle the ignorant and the research-averse. The conflict you run into here is that each magazine picks the same batch of players as their sleepers, be it a stud rookie running back, a third-year receiver primed to break out for a monster year, or a star looking to rebounding from a disappointing season. So by the time fantasy drafts roll around, everyone who did a modicum of preparation takes these players long before they should. Then the sleepers seldom deliver the big year that was promised. And you end up hating the player when you should really hate yourself.

Fantasy football magazines also operate on the assumption that there is little to no volatility in player output from year to year, which is obviously ridiculous in a league where turnover is constant. According to them, whoever was hot the year before will remain hot, while whoever sucked will still be DeAngelo Williams. How did that guy get good so quickly? Some concessions must be made to the powers of random events. Certainly there's no way to foresee injuries to major players, unless you have a good arrangement with a clairvoyant.

The dirty secret is that everyone is just as clueless as everyone else. Convincing yourself that you're more informed than others is a pleasant fiction. Don't fall into that trap. Save yourself the money and the trouble. The NFL offers the fan ample opportunities to squander money.

The one exception is a recent version of *Pro Football Prospectus*. Sure, it completely botches a prediction every once in a while—its evaluation of Wes Welker before he had a breakout season with New England in 2007 comes to mind—but the book is chock-full of invaluable knowledge, even some so arcane that you might base your selections on the quality of a team's training staff, which, though grounded in reason, is going way, way overboard. Unless, again, it's a big money league. Then no amount of preparation is too much.

VI.6 A Letter to Brian Westbrook Regarding His Questionable Playing Status for Sunday

Dear Brian Westbrook,

Even though I hate the Eagles and everything they stand for (being huge dicks, I think, is a major credo), I've enjoyed immensely the production you've given my fantasy team this season. I don't think I'm being out of line when I say that you are among the better first-round picks I've had in some time. The 26 points you gave me in Week 7 against Seattle got me over the hump in a game I needed to win to stay in playoff contention.

Because you are one of the league's premier receiving backs, so much of Philadelphia's offense flows through you. This makes a particularly appealing fantasy selection. Even if a stout defense is keying on the run against your team, there's still a good chance that you will rack up decent stats because of your ability to catch passes coming out of the backfield.

I have to say, however, that there is one habit of yours that has caused me some distress. I speak in reference to your tendency to sustain minor injuries, not practice all week, be listed as questionable for the following game, then downgraded to doubtful, then said to be a game-time decision (causing me enough concern that I put you on the bench thinking that, even if you play, it won't be much)—only for you to play the entire game, run for 150 yards, and score two touchdowns.

LISTEN FUCKTARD, EITHER MAKE IT CRYSTAL CLEAR THAT YOU INTEND TO PLAY OR I WILL SODOMIZE YOU WITH A KATANA. GOING THROUGH THIS SHIT EACH AND EVERY WEEK IS CAUSING ME TO DEVELOP A BITCH OF AN ULCER. I WILL RAKE YOUR EYES WITH A RUSTY NAIL, YOU DECEPTIVE SHIT-EATING CUNTWICH!

That is to say, I find this habit to be most irksome.

This week, again, I noticed you've sustained a calf injury that casts doubt on your status for Sunday. I understand that this is typically an injury that would create some difficulty for a running back. It is not a position in which it is easy to perform well at less than 100 percent. Officially, I see that you are listed as questionable, which means there is still a 50-50 chance that you could play. In keeping tabs on your status throughout the week, I see that head coach Andy Reid has said that you only went through limited practice on Friday and that your condition will be evaluated during warm-ups on Sunday.

HOLY FUCKING CRUSTY CUMBUCKET, BRIAN! DO YOU THINK I HAVE A SOURCE IN THE EAGLES' LOCKER ROOM? DO YOU

THINK I WANT TO WAIT BY MY COM-
PUTER ALL DAY SUNDAY FOR THE REPORT
ON WHETHER YOU'RE GOING OR NOT? DO
YOU THINK EVERYONE WHO ISN'T AN NFL
PLAYER HAS TIME FOR THESE THINGS,
YOU SELFISH ASS?

Due to injuries to my other running backs, my
bench is pretty thin at the moment. This game will
go a long way toward determining whether my team
makes the playoffs in my league. I would appreciate
having a chance to recoup the fifty-dollar entry fee I
paid at the beginning of the season. My friend, asshole that he is, has already acquired your backup,
Correll Buckhalter, making him primed to collect
what should be rightfully my points should you not
be able to start on Sunday. If, in fact, you will not
be playing, I need to know this ahead of time, so I
can pull a quick trade for another back.

DON'T THINK IT'S THAT HARD TO
LOOK UP YOUR ADDRESS ON THE INTER-
NET! I BET I CAN GOOGLE THAT SHIT REAL
EASY! JUST YOU WAIT! IF YOU COST ME
THIS GAME, I'LL GARROTE YOU IN YOUR
SLEEP WITH PIANO WIRE, BURY YOU IN
DOGSHIT, AND LIGHT IT ON FIRE! DOG-
SHIT BURNS OKAY JUST SO LONG AS YOU
POUR SOME GASOLINE ON IT! AND I HAVE
PLENTY OF GASOLINE, BRIAN!

I hope we can reach a speedy resolution as it
pertains to these lingering issues. Our association,
I think, has been a beneficial one, and I would like
for it to continue as such. Also, I don't want to go to
prison for killing you. I hear bad things.

Now, if you'll excuse me, I have to go write the
same letter to Willie Parker. Then mail a letter
bomb to Mike Shanahan for the whole running–
back-by-committee thing.

Yours in Christ,
Every Brian Westbrook Fantasy Owner

VI.7 Issue Threats to People Who Veto Your Fantasy Trades

The world of fantasy football is one of cutthroat games-
manship. Accordingly, you've got to cut some fucking
throats to get ahead, especially if it causes one of those
amazing arterial sprays. Because of the fierce competition
that marks fantasy, trades are a particularly sensitive
maneuver. The implications they have on the standings
mean any proposed transaction is scrutinized in a manner
so stringent it would make Supreme Court nominees
cringe.

The need for this process is manifest. When a fantasy
owner who is impossibly out of contention offers up his
best player to another owner who is in the thick of a title
run, it's time for the others in the league to rise up and bel-
lyache until that trade gets invalidated. For such a transac-

tion may put the beneficiary on the road to a league title due to the collusion of the down-and-out owner who has nothing to play for.

Often, though, when you find yourself on the business end of these refusals, which are done either by a vote of the majority of clenched-rectum owners in your league or the sole ruling of an imperious power-mad commissioner, no one can blame you for being aggrieved at the spite of others who were not savvy enough to rip off a suffering fantasy owner whose hope is lost but whose willingness to fuck others over remains startlingly intact. If you can coax a dying man to fork over his best assets before he expires, it is your right, nay, your obligation to do so. And, once having acquired those assets, the act of turning them on others as an instrument of fantasy football doom is enough to give you a glorious hate erection (these are the only kind Bill Belichick gets) for weeks.

Examples of lopsided trades are not always clear-cut, mind you. Not every rejected trade is as obviously rigged as Jabar Gaffney for Clinton Portis and Drew Brees. In many instances, people will overrule your trades even when they are relatively evenhanded. In such cases, an iron fist is required to guide these deals through the approval period.

Forcing through your proposed trades is going to take all of your cunning and all of your diplomatic dexterity, as well as an unstinting capacity for malevolence. The other owners in your league need to learn to fear your wrath, lest they get in their minds that it's okay to veto your deals, just because your stand to gain Steve Slaton and Matt Forte in a keeper league for a kicker. Let them worry about their business.

Try mailing any of the following sample threats to fellow owners in your league once one of your trades has been submitted for their approval. Be sure to cut all the ill-fitting letters out of various magazines, not so much to conceal the source of the letters (everyone knows they're from you) but because it makes you look cinematically deranged. And everyone knows actual crazy people love to copy the tactics of crazy people from movies.

- "Approve my fucking trade of Greg Camarillo for Brandon Marshall or I'll bayonet you in the nuts. My antique weapons collection has been itching for some use. If I forgot to get the rust off first, what's the difference?"

- "You know that scene in *Fargo* where the dude gets fed into the wood chipper? Well, approve my trade or I'll kick the shit out of you and then go watch that movie and laugh about what I've done."

- "Do you like pits of serpents? Shit, you weren't supposed to say yes. Well, once I find out what animal you're deathly afraid of, I fill the pit with that. And in you'll go!"

- "I'll chain you to a radiator and force-feed you Grady Jackson FUPA sweat."

- "Tank Johnson lent me his weapons cache and I've only gone through a couple dozen grenades. That still leaves thousands more, fuckstick."

- "Only interested in keeping things fair, you say? Well, I'm only interested in jamming a scalding fire poker in your eye."

- "Five words: live wire in your urethra."

- "Once I'm done with you, they'll never find the body. Unless investigators follow the lengthy list of obvious clues I leave in my wake."

- "If you don't think I can transfer flesh-eating bacteria over an Internet chat, you aren't paying attention to your rapidly disappearing midsection."

- "You know that Wu-Tang track where Method Man says he's gonna staple your asshole shut and keep feeding you? Well, I'll do the same thing, except I'll be feeding you gasoline."

- "Ever had your lower lip nailed to a railroad track? Well, it'll stay that way so long as you're smart enough to keep your trap shut about my acquisition of DeAngelo Williams for Drew Bennett."

- "I think a daytrip to the mountains could help us clear our heads and settle our differences. Sucks for you that I'll be dragging you from the back of my truck on the way there."

- "Ever had your head slammed in a car door? Well, I don't have a car, so you'll have to settle for a regular door."

A few of these and you'll have your trade clear with no fuss at all. Sure, you'll get booted out of the league for improper conduct, but if you were in a league that doesn't permit wanton threats of violence, you weren't doing the fantasy experience justice in the first place. Also, don't include threats over e-mail. The less evidence to present to the cops, the better. It's just common sense.

A Fan for All Seasons

VII.1 Seventeen Weeks of Sweet Delusion

For most fans, the football season is an endless stream of gut-punches and curb-stompings, interspersed with the odd moment of deceptive euphoria. But in the heady days of early September before that first kickoff, all is still joy and wonder. Now is time for the airing of the unreasonably bold prognostications! 19-0! 19-0! After all, there is parity in the league. Sweet, sweet parity. Which means any team that builds chemistry, stays healthy, and gets a lucky bounce here and there can go from 6-10 one year to 13-3 the next, no sweat. Will this necessarily occur? Probably not. But what's important is that it has the potential to occur. And that's the sad hope you'll stubbornly cling to like Tony Sparrano does to the Wildcat Formation.

Week 1—The opening game of the NFL season is exponentially more important than that of any other professional sport. The sixteen-game schedule amplifies the significance of any regular season contest compared to an eighty-two or, god forbid, a 162-game season. In the NFL, careers can be made and undone in single weeks. A Week 1 win can be the springboard to the top of the heap. Or it can be a misleading precursor to a horrible joke of a season. Either way, everybody wants to start the year on a positive note.

Week 2—Oh, no, your team lost on Kickoff Weekend! You're already in the hole after one game. The club is tied for last place in the division, for Pete Rozelle's sake! Breathe deep. Give your balls a reassuring pat. One loss isn't going to screw the season. In fact, sometimes teams need to lose to expose fixable flaws in the game plan and to keep players humble. There are good types of losses, or so you repeat to your bloodshot eyes in the mirror at 3 a.m.

Week 3—Analysts begin ticking off the short list of teams that have made the Super Bowl following an 0-2 start. The recitation of this fact scares you to the sphincter. A must-win game in September? Here goes . . .

Week 4—"Oh, God, oh, shit, the team is 0-3. All is lost. All. Is. Fucking. Lost. The plane has flown into the mountain! Someone direct me to the tallest building with a street-level awning unlikely to cushion my fall. But, wait, what? The 1998 Buffalo Bills made the playoffs after an 0-3 start? So . . . there's still hope? Yeah! You're right. I mean, sure they've lost all their games, but they were all closely contested. They can right this ship!"

Week 5—Doom and gloom falls heavy on fans of the 0-4 team. By now, you've put up Craigslist ads shopping your tickets for the rest of the season and considered developing a second drinking problem. What's more, the team becomes the butt of every gag on the pregame shows. Wearing your team's jersey in public is suddenly a more daunting prospect. As is listening to the haunting voices in your head.

Week 6—Hey, your team got its first victory of the season. Happy day! You get to show your face in public again. Vegas still has your guys as a touchdown underdog next week at home, so you know it's a tough road ahead, but there's a sign of life. Might want to power down the suicide machine for a spell.

Week 7—Back-to-back wins piques your delusional demons. For the time being, it's also sharply reduced the amount of the furniture you've ripped up around the house in fits of frustration. The thought, just maybe, that the team has turned it around creeps into your head.

Week 8—Another win and now the team has reached the bye week. After enduring a painful start at the beginning of the year, you've become very guarded with your optimism. You don't know if you're ready to commit to that kind of fever pitch again so soon. You promise to sleep under your team comforter one night just to see how it goes. Nothing serious.

Week 9—You're geared up for a second-half-of-the-season stretch run. This is the time of year that the great teams get it together and start owning shit. Meanwhile, your spirits are building, your ulcer has gone away, and the wife and kids are relieved enough by your calmer demeanor to move back into the house.

Week 10—The team has scaled its way out of the hole and back to a .500 record. They're right in the hunt. This season could go either way. Which is doing wonders for your chemical imbalance.

Week 11—ZOMFG! Five wins in row! The team has a winning record. Fire up the bandwagon. Start looking into making reservations at the Super Bowl host city. Flood online sports message board with trash-talk. Any small talk you enter into with strangers or store clerks should be about the team and its turn of good fortune. Let the karma gods know you appreciate their work.

Week 12—And just like that, all that good energy goes to shit as the team snaps its five-game win streak, taking all the wind out of its sails and the record back to .500. They'll have to run the table at this point. Right about now, "poison the drinking water" doesn't sound like the worst idea your grief-stricken mind has fed you all day.

Week 13—Yet another loss and the season is officially coming undone, as are the lingering threads of your sanity. The wife has gone back to sleeping at her sister's place. Meanwhile, you stare dead-eyed at the television while consuming bag after bag of bacon dust. Over the span of four days, you have three lengthy conversations about cosmology with your DVD remote.

Week 14—The team ekes out a win just to toy with you. Feeling emotionally spent at this point, you're too numb to notice you haven't left the house in three weeks. To your credit, you have been showering, even if that has consisted of standing in an ice-cold shower stream while crying for an hour. Clean is clean.

Week 15—What's this? Another win? For us? Huzzah! At 7-6, your team has put a decent enough season together to be on the outer reaches of the playoff hunt. And, if only they can win their final three games, and maybe get a little help, they'll squeeze into that last Wild Card spot! Maybe it's not too early to start lining up for the post–Super Bowl parade.

Week 16—Well, damn it all to fucking hell. Faced with the gauntlet and the team couldn't even win the first game of the final stretch. Now, with two weeks remaining, the team has already been eliminated from playoff contention. At this point, the question becomes whether it's acceptable to root for your team to lose so that it improves the team's draft order. It's a thorny question. If, say, the pick in question is first pick of the draft and the team has only won one game all year, it's fine to root against them, if only for the added comedic effect of total ineptitude. However, if you're only talking about the difference between the fifteenth and twelfth pick, that's not worth a dive against a hated division rival that's fighting for its own playoff life. You've got to ruin their shit.

Week 17—Few things are more depressing to the sports fan than the beginning of a postseason in which your team is not involved. It's a soul-flattening sensation of inconsequence. You get to watch all of these teams who, even if they lose, get to matter on the big stage. You'd much rather your team have a chance to go down fighting, or choking, as the case would be for Dallas.

The year ends on a dispiriting note. On the plus side, your team's coach will soon be fired (if he hasn't been already) and the search for his successor will take most of the next few weeks, leaving the eventual replacement not enough time to install his system, dooming him for obvious failure. Good times!

But if your team did, in fact, make the playoffs, well then calloo callay for you, dickface. Everything must be all smiles and cheeseburgers in the land of happy, you gloating sack of shit. Real fans are always fans! Even when the team indicates through years of inaction on the free-agent market that it isn't serious about winning but still wants a new stadium funded by public money, we'll be there for them. That's what fans do! And besides, we'll get to you front-runners soon enough.

VII.2 Strategies for a Losing Season:
Blame All Parties Involved

Jilted lovers, grieving families, dispossessed monsoon victims, quadruple amputees—tragic cases, all. But we can all agree these sob stories pale in comparison to the plight of the sports fan who cheers on a loser. Every day this wretched creature is buffeted by trash-talk from the fans of thriving teams and the expectation of another wrenching loss coming down the pike. The abject agony he must endure is tantamount to no other form of grief in the human condition. Save the blue balls, maybe.

What relief has he, this depantsed and downtrodden fan of the fallen? Some console themselves with the far-off promise of the hardly guaranteed glory of high draft choices. Others turn to the bottle, the needle, the bong, the moonshine jug, or the contents of a broken-into CVS pharmacy.

At best, those are short-term fixes, and they are ultimately placebos when compared to the real cure, that being the identifying and demonizing of a scapegoat. Though most bad teams have deficiencies at several key positions, it is the fan's job to distill the blame and fire it with a laserlike precision and a neutron-bomb-level intensity at one culpable individual. Is it fair? Hardly. But I'll be damned if it isn't reassuring to gang up on somebody.

The scapegoat can be any member of the team, though it usually falls on the shoulders of a high-profile individual, whether it be the starting quarterback, the head coach, the offensive or defensive coordinator, or the general manager. For another figure to get the glare of blame flashed on them, they must really, really turn on the suck. Adam Archuleta and Brian Russell are shining beacons in that respect.

Once labeled a scapegoat, it's next to impossible for that impression to be overturned. Lions fans, expert losers that they are, for years laid the blame for their franchise's string of failures at the feet of general manager Matt Millen. Some observers would describe their animosity as misplaced. All Millen did was hire inept coaches, sign mediocre players, squander first-round picks drafting bust receiver after bust receiver, and generally infect every level of the organization with the distinct aroma of disgrace and festering llama shit. But c'mon, what do you want from the guy? Competence?

Though the scapegoat deserves hate, fueled with the energy of a thousand suns, stay away from the personal when lashing out. Such attacks do nothing but make you look petty and unhinged, when you only mean to be petty and vengeful. Take, for example, the years when Steelers fans, disgusted with the erratic play of Kordell Stewart, circulated rumors that the quarterback was gay. Which is silly, because all quarterbacks are at least a little gay.

Once the scapegoat is identified, the fan's job is to make his life a living hell. The slightest misstep by the scapegoat is to be greeted with a heinous chorus of boos so vicious it could cripple the emotions of the most steeled individual. The scapegoat should be made to fear showing his face in public, more so than any other famous athlete already does. Call-in radio shows, blog entries, and comment sections on online newspaper articles should be flooded with invective against this cretin. Ignore pleas from the punditry for reason or temperance. Remind them that it is you, the fan, who pays this player's or coach's salary, and that this gives you the right to inflict undue misery.

To further the effect on the scapegoat, organize protests outside the stadium for his immediate benching or outright release. Be sure to alert the media and make costumes so wild and elaborate they put IMF protesters to shame. If your demands are still not heeded, coordinate mass walkouts during games. Sure, the ownership is still getting your money, but you're totally sticking it to them. Symbolism means more to billionaires slavishly monitoring the bottom line than you might think.

When the scapegoat is finally cut loose, celebrate wildly as though an albatross has finally been removed from your shoulder and a wondrous new era is being ushered in. Watch as the team loses a few more games, then find another scapegoat and repeat as necessary until a championship is won.

VII.3 Drink Deep of the Haterade, That Cool, Refreshing Drink

When you find yourself in the throes of an abortive season, there is nothing that can console you quite like the sweet succor of pure, unvarnished hatred. Hatred for your rivals. Hatred for the teams that are true contenders.

Hatred for the same passel of commercials that have been running all season long. It is this hatred that will sustain you through times of extreme fanial strife. Antipathy is top-shelf booze for the psyche.

In the years when your team is getting taken to the woodshed on a weekly basis, by mid-September you will already have it in your head that once again this isn't your season. Try not to take it too hard. But do take it hard on those who have it good. This is the way most seasons will work themselves out. The sooner you adjust yourself to failure, the sooner you can start focusing on discrediting the accomplishments of others.

Hatred gets a bad rap from those sportsmanship hucksters, but it is really nothing to fear. Without this eminently vital emotion, we'd be inclined to respect and honor the deeds of those we heartily dislike. I'm not sure that's a world any of us want to live in. Football is not built on mutual respect. Honor is shared among thieves. Fans deal in contempt and spite.

Hatred is stoked by the consumption of haterade, a potent elixir that is equal parts bile and spleen. Lucky for you haterade is a naturally occurring part of alcoholic drinks, and can easily be consumed alongside your usual drinking regiment.

Supping from the font of haterade, you will learn that there is not a great performance that you cannot undermine. If a team you dislike happens to benefit from a critical penalty that springs it to victory, you're more than entitled to harp on how lucky that team was to be the beneficiary of that bit of officiating. If a freakish bounce goes their way, never let that team's fan base believe for a second that their team earned that victory. When they do reach a title game, carp that the Super Bowl is boring and that no one wants to watch them, causing ratings to plummet. Even if the team wins decisively, there are useful outs for the hater. For instance, say the team you hate fails to cover a huge line they are given against an overmatched opponent. That only serves to show that they are hopelessly overrated. Even in victory you've got them feeling like shit.

Indeed, no claim is a closer friend to the hater than that of being overrated. Every fan presumes that his team is, at best, correctly appraised by the general population. The function of the hater is to show the flaws in that perception. The weapons are subtle, but many. For starters, if the hated team is a Wild Card making a run to a championship, surely they lost to some embarrassing squads in the regular season. Why, how good could the team be if they lost to the Bears in Week 16? It's important to point this out to their fans ad infinitum, even over their fans reasonable objection that the loss only came when they were resting their starters for the playoffs.

If all that fails, there's always the refuge of insulting the stereotypes of a team's fan base. Is it the Packers? Then they're fat, ugly cheesebilly Favretards. The Steelers? Unemployed mouthbreathing rag twirlers. The Patriots?

Pfft. Boston's really a baseball town. A racist-ass baseball town. And everybody has AIDS. And their AIDS stink. Don't forget the Cowboys. You'd have to take a pestle to my frontal lobe to make me as dumb as a Cowboys fan.

The levelheaded fan who doles out respect to a successful team doesn't exist. No team is unobjectionable in the eyes of a fan of a losing squad. This is the trap that ensnares fans of successful teams. They assume that other teams' fans will embrace the positive qualities of their team as they make their run at history. Boston fans, in particular, are guilty of this. It's a fundamental fan fallacy. No one wants to give another team its due. That's simply the nature of fandom. Expecting any different of rival fans, no matter how sympathetic you may think your own team is, is the height of douchiness. Stow that shit and enjoy your title run. Don't look for validation from other fan bases. You aren't gonna get it.

The key to hating is not to let the people know that you hate them. This takes a bit of loathsome finesse. Otherwise you come off looking like an irrational curmudgeon who is out to piss on the parades of others. Even if that is exactly what you are doing, you can't let them know that, or else it lessens the effect of your slurs. Proper hating takes years of practice to master, but once you get it down, you can apply it to fields independent of sport. Coworkers, in-laws, strangers who make you feel bad about yourself. All of them can be the focus of your burning disgust. You'll find hatred's the best coping mechanism you can't get from a doctor. Unless you finagle a medical marijuana prescription. That can help you deal with anything.

7.4 When "Wait 'Til Next Year" Is an Annual Mantra, or the Fan Bases of the Damned

Either through the unfortunate vagaries of inheritance or through the grievous impulsiveness of youth, you may find yourself linked to an ineffably, monstrously inept team. How this happens is one of the confounding mysteries that fate likes to stir in the stew of life with its unwashed pinky finger.

Sure, on some level you can enjoy the league as a whole, as a beleaguered student of the game, but you are condemned to view the NFL from the bottom up. You are but fools, doomed forever to the caste of losers. A wretched band of untouchables bound to serve the good teams the wins they desire. Their seasons begin with inflated hopes, flying in the face of reason, and terminate well before the actual season is over with crushed dreams and crying jags.

While there are many teams that are marked by pitiful performance on the field, there exists a fetid threesome that tests the mettle of their fans in ways only war refugees can understand. Despite fielding a team throughout the entirety of the modern era, they have yet to reward their faithful with so much as an appearance on the grandest of stages, the Super Bowl. Meanwhile, the Panthers and the Ravens made it to the big dance in their first decade of operation. Nobody said fandom was fair.

The New Orleans Saints, the Detroit Lions, and the Cleveland Browns. If ever there was a three-headed hell-hound of fail, it is they. Fans of the Lions and Browns gripe that their teams won championships prior to the Super Bowl era, but that's like saying you're rich because you have fifteen million drachmas. Championships won before the advent of the Super Bowl are a trivial footnote of history.

On a side note, the Jacksonville Jaguars and the Houston Texans also belong on the list of teams that have failed to reach the Super Bowl; however, considering that these franchises are respectively fourteen and seven years old, it's a bit unfair to hold them to the same standards as these three perennial tonguers of cornhole. Additionally, they have it rough enough living in Jacksonville and Houston without more ribbing.

One could also include Chargers fans, even though the team has made one Super Bowl appearance, seeing as how no pro team from San Diego has ever won a major sports title. But then again, the weather is too nice for anyone to really be miserable there. Nuts to those lucky, well-tanned jerkwheats.

If there's any glimmer of deceptive hope for these teams, it is that a longtime member of their circle of futility, the Arizona Cardinals, has recently be expunged from their ranks with an appearance in Super Bowl XLIII. Naturally, the sudden success of a fellow eternal NFL punch line should give them cause to believe in their own chances, but no, it's only a bitter reminder that even the Arizona Cardinals can win and they can't.

Here is a breakdown of their collective woes. Don't skip past. It's not too sad. They're still slightly less depressing than the latest Holocaust drama you got from Netflix.

New Orleans Saints

Despite having the Superdome famously ravaged by a hurricane, the NFL continued to force this team to play what were considered home games on neutral fields after the stadium was fixed. So it's not only fate that hates them. Meanwhile, owner Tom Benson would just prefer all their games be played in Los Angeles. And of course, they had the privilege to root for Papa Manning rather than his Super Bowl–winning brood. Punch yourself in the nuts again, Saints fans, before the universe has another chance to.

Relevant Fail-toids

- The team was in operation for thirty-three years before winning its first playoff game following the 2000 season. They then won their second following the 2006 season, so you could say things are looking up.
- Has had two quarterbacks named Billy Joe (Billy Joe Hobert and Billy Joe Tolliver) start games for them. One is one too many.
- Had grating "Who Dey" chant stolen by the lowly

Cincinnati Bengals. Still seeking restitution or government aid.

Suggested additional self-torture (because once you get a taste for it, you can never have enough) for Saints fans: Change your name to Billy Joe. Wait for next hurricane. Stay put.

Detroit Lions

Not only do the Lions administer unspeakable pain to their own fans, but they do harm to the rest of America with their shitty play by being one of two teams, along with the Dallas Cowboys, that tradition demands always have a game on Thanksgiving. They are spared from being the most embarrassing team in all sports only by the illogical devotion of their fans.

Relevant Fail-toids

- Where to start? There's always the matter of them losing all sixteen of their games last season. That's a good jumping off point.
- In twenty-one attempts, the team has never won a game at Washington. Their last victory on the road against the Redskins came in 1935, when the franchise was the Boston Redskins.
- Went three consecutive seasons (2001–2003) without a victory on the road, a first in NFL history.

- Barry Sanders, the greatest player in the history of this or perhaps any team, opted to retire at the age of thirty—when he could have played several more years and only needed about 1,500 yards to surpass Walter Payton's career rushing record—rather than play any longer for such an utterly impotent organization.

Suggested additional self-torture for Lions fans: Wear a throwback Matt Millen Raiders jersey to Ford Field.

Cleveland Browns

Like Detroit, enjoys a base of masochistically loyal supporters. Possessed an inopportune dynasty with Jim Brown, likely the greatest player ever, prior to the modern era. Better way too early than never, eh, Cleveland?

Relevant Fail-toids

- A key contributor to the forty-five-year Cleveland sports title drought. Admittedly, the squalid town doesn't bear the fertile soil needed for a championship yield.
- "Red Right 88" and "The Fumble." While other teams give names to their successes ("The Catch"), the Browns memorialize their bitter failures.
- Lost the franchise to Baltimore in 1996. The Baltimore Ravens proceeded to win a Super Bowl four years later. Browns fans still picture Modell laughing at them when trying to have sex. Hopefully this prevents breeding.

Suggested additional self-torture for Browns fans: Jump in the Cuyahoga River, light it on fire.

VII.5 The Week Between the Conference Championships and the Super Bowl Is the Tool of the Devil (as Well as the Networks, Which Are Run by the Devil)

Among the more odious phenomena that blight the football landscape—besides the ever-present scourge of bandwagon fans and the fact that there are timeouts after scores and kick returns—is the two-week break between the conference championships and the Super Bowl. What purpose does this serve other than to dull the excitement that's been building to a fever pitch throughout the playoffs? To hype the Super Bowl? Because surely the hundreds of millions of people who tune in to this cultural institution wouldn't bother unless they had two full weeks of soft-focus player profiles and puff pieces crammed down their gullets. Nope. Not a one of them.

Not only does the two-week break impose a needless calm in the middle of the frenzied postseason, it destroys any momentum a team may have built up through January, bores fans to tears, and hurts the quality of the Super Bowl itself. Only seven times in its forty-three-year history has the Super Bowl been held the week after the conference title games, with the margin of victory being noticeably smaller during the one-week games than the standard two-week ones.

Of those seven Super Bowls, three of them were decided

on the final play: Scott Norwood's kick-starting four years of Bills Super Sunday suffering in January 1991; Kevin Dyson getting tackled a yard shy of the goal line in the Rams' 23–16 victory in Super Bowl XXXIV; and Adam Vinatieri's winning kick to complete the Patriots upset of those same Rams in Super Bowl XXXVI.

The one-week games also give a fighting chance to the underdog, who, coming in with a full head of steam, has a legitimate shot against a daunting opponent. The Redskins' 27–17 comeback win over the Dolphins in Super Bowl XVII, and Kansas City's 23–7 upset victory over Minnesota in Super Bowl IV were examples of this. In fact, only two of the one-week games have been blowouts: Dallas's 30–13 bludgeoning of Buffalo in Super Bowl XXVII (though the Bills led at halftime), and the last Super Bowl played with the one-week interim, the Tampa Bay Buccaneers' 48–21 victory over the Oakland Raiders in Super Bowl XXXVII (though the Raiders were four-point favorites entering the game).

After holding three of the four Super Bowls between the 1999 and 2002 seasons with the one-week break, the league reestablished the two-week layover beginning with the 2003 season. There are plenty of rational arguments as to why the two-week break is detrimental to the big game, but none more so than that it's excruciating torture for fans, an echo chamber of unsubstantial hype that political conventions could only ever dream to be.

Moving the Pro Bowl to fill this gap, which will begin

starting next year, does exactly nothing to alleviate the dull that settles in the lull. It just means even more players will opt to take the game off. And that the Pro Bowl, as devoid of meaning as it already is, will somehow become even more pointless.

A two week buildup is an agonizing dog-and-pony show that's nigh on unwatchable. For the first week, neither team has even arrived in the host city, forcing bloviating pundits to fill the vacuum with the sickliest scraps of rumor and warmed-over analysis to ratchet up the hype to obscene heights. Is a starting linebacker being limited in practice one day? Best sound the doomsday siren! Has a reserve player said in an interview that he's confident in his team's chances? Oooooooeeeee, that's bulletin board material right there! Sounds like somebody's guaranteeing a win! Will he be the next Namath? It's enough to make you watch hockey.

Eventually the second week rolls around and the teams make their arrival, an event which, in keeping with the shitshow nature of the two-week break, is breathlessly covered by the media. Footage of people walking on an airport tarmac has never been so captivating. Yet no network will refuse to show it like it's massive breaking news, as though the prospect of air travel suddenly became doubly perilous with the coming of the Super Bowl.

At some point the mayors of the participating cities (or, in the case of Jacksonville, sparsely civilized midden heaps) will wager items that are symbolic of their hometowns. If it's Philadelphia, it's probably a cheesesteak. If it's Baltimore, it's spent casings found at a crime scene. What's most galling is that everyone looks the other way during this brazen disregarding of gambling laws. I should be able to wager foodstuff if I so choose. And if I instead substitute the money used to buy food in my bets, so be it. Innocent fun!

On Tuesday of the second week comes Super Bowl Media Day, where the players are made available to the press, but only after they've been strictly admonished by their coaches not to say anything remotely interesting. Even the most charismatic player won't do much more than taunt desperate reporters in need of a juicy quote. Every possible human interest story will be mined for copy, regardless of the player's spot on the roster. Does a player have a crazy hobby or a sick relative? Well, they're getting a fifty-inch profile in a Sunday paper somewhere around the country. To the relief of all involved, inevitably some wacky female foreign reporter will spice things up by showing up in a wedding dress and trying to propose to one of the quarterbacks. The QB politely demurs with a chuckle before taking her from behind in the hotel an hour later. Unless it's Kurt Warner. He'll just take her to Bible study.

The bleakness of the off-season; it is where fandom goes to die and hope is crushed underfoot. It looms ever closer. So, as tedious as the extra week off is, you must savor it, no matter how forced the joy. In a few short weeks, you'll kill even for this.

VII.6 If You Need Don Cheadle to Motivate You for the Playoffs, You Aren't a Fan

Oh, la di da, loogit you, fan of a team that made it to the postseason. Aren't you living high on the hog? Well, snaps to you, fortunate fanboy. Your team has succeeded in stumbling into the playoffs. They're now only a few perilous clambering steps from the mountaintop. What are you willing to do to propel them the rest of the way?

Can you rise to the occasion of the postseason? Are you prepared for an entire month of wearing the same lucky underwear, peeing on the same lucky bush, and jerking it to the same lucky picture of Lucy Pinder? Good. Because whatever's been working for you throughout the year has to be your MO during the run to the Super Bowl. This is no time to waver in your routine. Every behavior from Monday to Friday now becomes immutable from week to week. Let no amount of OCD be enough. The slightest deviation from your path could result in devastation.

In January, your team is counting on you for no less than the totality of your being. That includes all of it, along with, like, your philtrum, duodenum, and mastoid process. Even the several pounds of beef sitting in your intestines that will never be fully digested. You gotta put that to work too. No free rides! You've poured four months of your life into seeing this team into contention, and now, once they're at the doorstep of greatness, you must prove that your compulsion is strong enough to will them to the promised land.

Think I'm exaggerating? Indeed, your very health is at stake. Earlier this year a team of researchers from the Keck School of Medicine at the University of Southern California discovered that death rates in Los Angeles rose significantly the day the Rams lost the Super Bowl in 1980 and dipped the day the Raiders won the title in 1984. Can't poke holes in that methodology. It's rock-solid proof! YOUR LIFE IS ON THE LINE! CHEER, CHEER FOR YOUR LIFE!

Clichéd though the notion is, the truism stands that everything in the playoff is more intense. The pace is faster, the hits are harder, and fights in the stands are that much more likely to result in cracked crania. You too must respond in kind. Not for a moment should you let your guard down, and most definitely never let your beer down. Do you lose your voice for a day following a game? After a playoff game, it needs to move to three. With the season on the line each week from this point forward, nothing must impede the fan's focus. Every conversation must revolve around the fortunes of the team, and all concerted effort must go to making sure you don't invoke a dreaded jinx with a slip of the tongue that doesn't include "if" prior to a hypothetical situation about the team winning.

Have acquaintances who are fans of your team's next-round opponent? It is incumbent upon you to disassociate with them as quickly and as acrimoniously as possible. It is useless to attempt otherwise. Any continued relations will be torn asunder well before kickoff in a flurry of argument spittle and hurt feelings. It's better to call these things off before they get truly ugly. While regular season showdowns can be the stuff of friendly tiffs, playoff contests can drive an unbridgeable gap between the closest of relations. It just so happens that in January 1993, midway through the historic Bills comeback against the Oilers in the Wild Card game, a record three dozen marriages were dissolved as a direct result of the game. Granted, most of these were by virtue of murder-suicides committed by Oilers fans, but technically it holds true.

A word of advice to the backers of top teams: a first-round bye is no time to rest on the laurels of an impressive regular season. Indeed, even with the brief reprieve from the pressures of a do-or-die contest, the Wild Card weekend is not one to be taken lightly by the fan of a dominant team. Recent years have shown that the extra week of rest can make players rusty and ill-prepared to face the high-intensity pace of playoff football. The same can be said of fans. So keep yourself in game shape by getting ready to detest whichever squad emerges from the first round. Pretend-berate people in public to see how your game is holding up. If you get them to flee for their lives, you know you're getting where you need to be.

There are no easy answers for full playoff readiness. It's a tense, nerve-wracking experience for the fan, a trial for the senses. Some fans are clearly not ready for it and their inexperience shows. Remember Bengals fans after the 2005 season? They hadn't seen their team in the postseason in fifteen years, and they weren't able to keep from passing out long enough to see Carson Palmer's ACL torn to ribbons. After that, it was lights out all around Paul Brown Stadium. Imagine everything you're used to on a regular Sunday amped up to the nth degree. Except that you're cheering for your very football lives. Remember, elimination is tantamount to being consigned to the purgatory of an early off-season, all while consequential football is still being played. Knowing what's at stake, a grasp on sanity isn't a luxury you can afford.

7.7 Super Bowl Parties Are for Amateurs—but Still Worth It

Super Bowl Sunday is to football what St. Patrick's Day or New Year's Eve is to drinking: a nationally celebrated amateur hour. Everyone, whether they give a shit about the game or not, gathers around the TV for fellowship with friends at the altar of football's biggest stage. This is the holy day when all Americans, no matter how football resistant they may be, have to pay their respects to Stitchface, the polytheist god of football fandom and cowhide leather.

For many viewers, this is the only time all year they're going to be watching a football game. And it shows. They're only watching for the commercials, they declare, right before asking you what constitutes an illegal contact penalty. Be sure to demonstrate on their face. Sure, everyone is at least moderately interested in seeing the commercials, even if the vast majority of them are overlong, overly produced train wrecks brought down by the meddling hands of countless company execs. There're a couple with a monkey. There's five or six with a guy getting hit in the nuts. There's one with a guy getting hit in the nuts by a monkey while Fergie laughs in the background. Lather, rinse, retire to the kitchen for a beer.

Heaven forbid you actually have a vested interest in the game and be stuck in a crowd of casual or neutral viewers. You can't do it. After the first ugly looks they shoot you for being loud you'll want to burn the place down. Friends who know you from a non-sports context will want to discuss work or their lives or some other piddling shit you have no time for. The Super Bowl Party is a social event that has almost nothing to do with the game itself. Snubbing people on your Super Bowl Party guest list only because they lack a passion for the game is still considered every bit a harsh dismissal. Blowing them off for not bringing sufficiently good food or drinks is still blessedly legit, and therein you see where the casual football fan finds his use on this day: provider of grub.

There is a way to remedy the dearth of interest in the outcome of the contest. Have the host collect an entry fee from each person who arrives. Assign an equal number of attendees to be considered ad-hoc fans of each participating team for that night. If it appears to be a lopsided matchup, have people draw the teams out of a hat to prevent them from bitching at you for sticking them with the eventual losers. The fans of the team that prevails on the field get the kitty at the end of the night. This ensures, at a very least, rapt attention paid toward the game itself and little unrelated socializing.

Drinking games are also vital to the enjoyment of everyone on hand. These are difficult to create in the abstract without knowing which story lines broadcasters will ceaselessly cram down viewers' throats throughout the duration of the game. Worry not, you'll know them well in advance of the day of the game, as the NFL commentariat will have already been droning on about the grand conflict that looms over the contest for a week and change. And God help you if a star player has announced that the Super Bowl will be his final game, as John Elway and Jerome Bettis have done in the past. Basing your drinking game on mentions of that will render you dead from alcohol poisoning well before the seven-hour pregame show hits its halfway mark.

Another grating element to the Super Bowl is the metric assload of advertisers who refer to it as "the big game" in their product pushes. Naturally, there's a reason for this and it has to do with fat-ass sacks of cash. You see, the NFL has an exclusive trademark on the term Super Bowl and other phrases associated with the game, and its team of intellectual property rights lawyers isn't exactly keen on other companies employing those terms for commercial uses. In fact, the league tried to copyright "the Big Game" as well to no avail in June 2007. Enforcement of name usage isn't the NFL's only battleground, though. The league has tried to block church congregations from watching the game on mammoth TV screens, arguing that public exhibitions on screens larger than fifty-five inches are damaging to ratings. In many of these areas, the league has been successful in protecting its brand, even if it comes at the price of negative press.

Still, even if the people you have to watch the game with are clueless, the commercials suck, and the halftime show only appeals to geriatrics with poor taste in music, it's still an awesome spectacle to behold and, if it happens to be a good game, it can provide the height of the season's drama. Seeing a dramatic finish with the league's grandest prize on the line is just the thing to get you fired up for another season to kick off. Right. Fucking. Now. Except, screw you sideways, it's not coming until September and you've got seven Stitchface-forsaken months of barren baseball-filled spring and summer wasteland to occupy before that happens. Surviving the off-season is going to require a little help and a lot of drugs.

7.8 Celebrate a Title, Bitches!

Seeing your favorite team be victorious in the Super Bowl produces a feeling superior even to having an orgasm while you're stoned and watching your worst enemy drown in an enclosed tank of raw sewage. It really is that good. I might even be understating it. Yet polite society demands that we list our happiest moments in life as personal, family-type things, like the first time you meet your significant other or the birth of your children, but that's a bunch of treacly Hallmark horseshit. Your team's first title trumps both of those by about a parsec. Subsequent titles are ahead as well, though that distance is measured by mere light-years.

Once the initial delirium-fueled shrieking subsides, and you've emptied your tear ducts awkwardly onto the shoulder of the person next to you, it's time to launch into some serious celebration. You didn't suffer this long to settle for some light merriment. No, you're entitled, nay, obligated to tear the goddamn roof off and cause a ruckus. Because who knows if you'll ever get the opportunity again. Chances are you might not. You can't squander a situation that allows for socially acceptable mayhem. That goes beyond fan law. That's some fundamental life shit right there.

Get on the phone and drunk-dial everyone you know. Scream incoherently once you hear the other end pick up. They'll understand. Let them share in your ecstasy. Usually when you're boasting about your favorite team, you have to hold back for the sake of karma biting you in the ass. Well, not now. You just won the title. There's nothing to lose. Get outlandish with it.

Once you've blanketed your circle of friends in a tidal wave of braggadocio via texting and drunk-dialing, it's time to really get crazy. Commit a few felonies. Foster some future regrets. Go way the fuck overboard.

Riot! One consolation if you were too cheap to score Super Bowl tickets is that you'll be around for the unruly riot that immediately follows your team's victory. Even if they lose, there will probably be a riot. If you live in Oakland, this new riot will adjoin the riot already in progress, to form an über-riot that will take the National Guard weeks to quell. Bars will empty out with revelers into the downtown. Store windows will be smashed, cars overturned, ladies' virtues compromised. It's a giant bacchanalia the likes of which neither you nor the local news has never seen. Be sure to yell a slurred "number one" with an upheld finger into the camera. Bonus points if it's the middle finger. You'll want this moment recorded for posterity.

Parade. By the time the riot quiets down, it'll be right about time for the victory parade. Hundreds of thousands will descend on the parade route for some huddled jubilation in the winter weather. Your sense of joyous disbelief will keep you warm. That and all the alcohol still overwhelming your blood.

Winners deserve the week off work/victory lap and victory nap. It's enough of a travesty that the day after the Super Bowl is not a national holiday. The working world just assumes hangovers are going to cure themselves. What's more, the fans of the two Super Bowl participants need at least a week to recover from their team being in the game. So don't bother showing up for the next five days. If the boss has a

problem with it, calmly explain upon your return that
the job has your undivided attention for the next six
months. At least when you're not gazing lovingly at
the reflection in the mini Lombardi Trophy on your
desk.

Merch! A championship is the perfect excuse to
splurge on all-new team-sponsored swag. Swaddle
yourself in the spoils of your historic win. As the years
go by and it fades further into the past, the title will
seem more and more bittersweet. Therefore it's important to savor the win as much as possible while it's
fresh and unalloyed by failure.

Shit-talking becomes shit-gloating. What's the
point of winning a title if you can't be a dick and rub it
in everyone's face? That's almost a Buddhist koan. If a
team wins a title and no one shamelessly gloats about
it, did it really happen? I submit that it did not. So get
out there and make the world aware of your triumph.
Get thee to message boards and inundate them with
taunts. There's such a thing as a poor winner and you
know because you're it. Great feeling, no? Look at
those losers getting upset. Don't they wish they were
in your shoes.

Grace period? Not until after my three-peat! For
a fan of the new world champions (and kindly guzzle
meconium if you think it's wrong for Super Bowl winners to call themselves "world champions"), there are
several issues to consider. How much of a pass should

the coach and the quarterback get if they come out sucking the next year? How many years have to go by until you can get upset when they don't deliver another ring? ESPN's resident displaced Masshole Bill Simmons has argued that any champion should get a five-year grace period from its fans, that no matter what happens their followers aren't allowed to complain. Seems a mite bit generous, but being magnanimous is easy when winning is the norm. You'll find your patience wears thin in a hurry the first time a champion is crowned that isn't your team.

With so much elation, you'd think there wouldn't be a possibility of the downside. Oh, how wrong you are. Stuck in blissful intoxication, you didn't happen to notice the mounting collection of douches surrounding you to watch your team's games. You never bothered to notice them before, but they arrived in greater and greater numbers as the team crept toward greatness. Now that they're there, there's no getting rid of them. Your worst fears have been confirmed: your world championship team fan base has been overrun by bandwagon fans. Break out the flamethrower.

ARTICLE VIII

Surviving the Endless Off-Season

VIII.1 Your End of the Year Denial Is So Strong You'll Actually Watch a Part of the Pro Bowl

The dust has settled on the Super Bowl. The victory parade course has been traversed. The Super Bowl champion shirts premade for the team that lost have been shipped to Nicaragua. The Raiders have fired another coach. So concludes another glorious NFL season. This is when panic sets in. Seven whole months of football-less existence stares you dead in the face, like Shawne Merriman in mid-'roid rampage.

Being that it's the Al Davis–like death rattle of the NFL season, you'd think you would quaff down every moment of the Pro Bowl as if it were Marisa Miller's bath water, making certain not to squander the final vestiges of the game you will very soon be bereft of. But have you ever tried to do it? You can't. Not possible. For even the most rock-ribbed of football fans can't bring themselves to sit through this entire perfunctory spectacle. And with good reason. It's about as unwatchable as the People's Choice Awards, a Uwe Boll movie, and anything starring Eva Longoria wrapped in a box of suck.

Don't get me wrong. Many fans will give the Pro Bowl a shot. They'll tune in for about an offensive drive or two, hoping to spot one of their favorite players in the game. After all, it's usually a high-scoring affair and, hey, all the premiere stars are involved. Except the dozen or so who opted not to play because they're nursing phantom injuries or getting a jump start on their sex cruise through Asia. But that's it. You can't make it through any more than that. I challenge you to try. You'd fare better trying to keep a pack of Jets fans away from an exposed pair of tits.

The Pro Bowl is agonizing because it's so inconsequential. But that's no different from the all-star games in any other sport, even baseball with its pathetic attempt to inject significance into its All-Star Game by putting home field advantage in the World Series on the line. The NFL shows mercy (the league does not usually make a practice of this) by placing the Pro Bowl after the conclusion of the season. Why break up a riveting regular season with an empty exhibition smack dab in the middle, when no one wants to be part of it? Not that NFL players hate to be selected, mind you. They love the trip to Hawaii and the clause in their contract that triggers a huge pay day when they do get picked. It's the whole "exposing themselves to pointless injury" thing that possibly dampens their competitive fire for the Post–Super Bowl Classic.

Take the cautionary tale of Robert Edwards. He rushed for 1,115 yards as a rookie for the New England Patriots in 1998. (Note to Patriots fans: this is three years before you realized the team existed.) After the season, the running back blew out his knee and nearly bled to death in an all-rookie flag football game played on the beach at Waikiki days before the Pro Bowl. Edwards didn't play in the league again for another three years, playing one more season in the NFL in 2002 with the Dolphins before spending the rest of his professional career in the CFL. Yes, the CFL, a fate even worse than the Bengals. They might as well have put him down. Taking that in mind, can you blame the players for being a little less than amped to expose themselves to cataclysmic injury, even at the end of the year? Of course you can. Being blindly and unctuously judgmental is the right of every fan. But it's still something to consider.

Really, the only time the Pro Bowl is even halfway relevant is two months before the game is actually played, that is, when the rosters are officially released. This announcement gives pundits and talking heads a solid week of "Who got snubbed?" grist for the horseshit mill. Zealous homers get worked up over so-and-so not getting the nod and over which team got the most representatives. It's all eventually rendered pointless because, by the time the game rolls around, most of the players originally selected have pulled out and half the league ends up in Honolulu. Heck, play your cards right and you might even get an invite.

The Pro Bowl isn't without its draws. For one, you get to see the coaches of the teams that lost in conference title games suffer the humiliation of halfheartedly leading a squad of stars into pointless battle. The axiom is that no one remembers the loser of the Super Bowl, but that's not necessarily true. There have been several memorable Super Bowl meltdowns, not the least of which was Bill Belichick storming off the field with a second left in Super Bowl XLII. You can see the deep sea of dejection in their eyes. In HD it's quite compelling.

Then there's the custom of the Pro Bowl quarterbacks paying the way for their entire offensive line to go to Hawaii along with them. A heartwarming gesture, to be sure, but just think what a squandered opportunity that is. Why not the entire cheerleading squad? With the number of QBs each conference carries for the Pro Bowl, there could be any many as seven or eight squads on the premises during the game. That would provide for an ample number of cutaway shots to make the telecast palatable for perverted minds.

Though it's a deeply flawed and eminently irrelevant tradition, the Pro Bowl is all that stands between you and full-on football withdrawal, which begins to kick in sometime around 1 p.m. the following Sunday, when you shatter the phalanges in your hand mashing the buttons on the remote control in search of a game, any game. Alas, there are none to be found. You, sir, abject victim of the linear nature of time, are tragically ensconced in the void of the off-season. May God have mercy on your soul.

VIII.2 Feign an Interest in Other Sports and Other People

Learning to endure things you can't stand: it's one of the most vital skills any person can learn. And it's the only realistic shot the football fan has to outlast the gauntlet of unspeakable suffering that is the off-season. As smokers try to break the habit by turning to chewing gun, the football fan has to find wholly inadequate substitutes that only serve to remind how great football is. It's a bottomless stoma in the throat of suckage.

The temptation to turn inward and hibernate away this fallow period will be strong. But this is not a time to be alone. Seek the company of others. You'll have plenty of opportunities to shun them during football season. After all, companionship is a must when one feels bereft, mostly because they'll keep you from cutting yourself.

To be sure, it's a long slog, this off-season, a journey fraught with boredom, rife with sober thought, and sickeningly teeming with pointless conjecture about football with no action to refute or support it. A good time to get married, have children, do some work at the office. For the first few weeks, you will be haunted by the phantom pains of a Sunday without football, akin to what an amputee feels for a lost limb. Waking up hungover from a

Saturday night of hard-core liver poisoning, the grogginess becomes that much more uncomfortable and the Fatty Lumpkins waking up next to you that much uglier if football isn't fitting into the plans of the day.

Something then has to fill the void. Really, anything vaguely athletic and competitive will do. As flawed as all these alterna-sports can be, you'll just have to swallow them and find appealing aspects about their being. There's only so long you can watch replays of NFL games from the previous season before you're drooling half-naked on the basement floor banging Starting Lineup figures into one another and making Chris Berman–like spit-laden football onomatopoeias.

College Basketball—An oasis of thrilling competition, an even better one now that Billy Packer is gone. Now the sport is just a few more Dick Vitale vocal ulcers away from challenging the NFL as a captivating sports spectacle. Well, at least during its championship tournament.

NBA—Unlike the NFL, basketball players are permitted to exhibit an iota of flair in their play. And even celebrate a little. Also, clubs have dance teams, which are a fine analogue to cheerleaders.

Hockey—There's fighting, for one. The empty seats allow you to kick your legs up. And Patriots fans will appreciate the preponderance of white players.

Baseball—Um . . . hold on. I know I can think

of something. Gimme a sec. Perhaps watching an inning can stir some sort of pleasant recollection. No. Nonono. Four straight pick-off attempts by the pitcher when up by four runs with a runner on first? Here we go: fans look less obnoxious wearing baseball caps featuring the logos of baseball teams than they do wearing the incongruous caps featuring an NFL logo. There. I think that counts as praise.

One of the knottier questions about watching other sports is how to divide your allegiances. Ideally, you would proceed with rooting for all the teams in the same city as your favorite football team, as well as those of the nearest university with a prominent athletic program. But what if it's a city that doesn't have representation in other, lesser sports? For example, Seattle no longer has an NBA team, Baltimore has no NHL franchise, and Green Bay is lucky to have an Applebee's as a distraction outside the Packers.

Being a bandwagon fan in a lesser sport is no more tolerable than one in the football world. In fact, anyone who pulls for the rare combination of Yankees–Lakers–Cowboys–USC Trojans–Duke Blue Devils–Detroit Red Wings–Manchester United–Tiger Woods merits a flaming arrow in the rectum. Any two of that permutation entitles the banner chaser to a swift cattle prodding.

If you follow an NFL team located in a city where you don't live, adopting the other teams in that city prevents the unforgivable awkwardness that comes with explaining factitious rooting interests. Say that city lacks a franchise in a given sport. Then you have free rein to choose as you wish. Glomming onto the one located closest to your present residence is the classy way to go, though if you move you must definitively drop one team before selecting another. No cross-pollination of fandom will do. It's very absolutist that way. College sports can be determined at a young age, with cheering preference being given to a parent's alma mater or to the college you end up attending. Either way, liking Notre Dame makes you a fucktaster.

VIII.3 Oh, No! Your Favorite Player Left in Free Agency! Disown Him at Once!

That ungrateful cocksnot! How dare he accept a more generous contract from another franchise, just because it was a longer term deal than the one your team offered, with more guaranteed money and a clause that entitles him to two coke-caked strippers for every touchdown reception. Does loyalty toward an organization that drafted him and would cut him as soon as his production slipped mean nothing? Apparently not. Try not to let the disillusionment harsh your buzz.

The start of the free agency period is the first of the off-season pseudo-events, during which there is no football action but instead granules of news that give obsessives cause to breathlessly speculate about the impact of these transactions on a season that is still practically a lifetime away. The free agency period typically begins the first week of March, and stays remotely interesting for about two weeks until all the players of even marginal consequence have been signed to ludicrously bloated deals and the Raiders have offered a six-year, $50 million contract to a line cook at a Mexican restaurant. The Redskins, too, will reach terms with a player four years past his prime, goading their fans to pronounce the upcoming season yet another in which the Burgundy and Gold will stride effortlessly into Super Bowl lore—just like the past seventeen years.

Traditionalists contend that free agency robs fans of any emotional connection to their favorite team because the rate of turnover is so high that, with the exception of a few marquee players, the entire roster is usually overhauled every couple of years. With so few familiar faces, how could anyone really get attached to a team over the years? It's theory based in logic, but one that doesn't hold up well in the face of history, kind of like that communism thing. In the nearly two decades since the NFL instituted unrestricted free agency, fandom hasn't gotten any less intense. For the most part, fans would like their favorite players to be sympathetic, fully formed personalities they feel like they can get to know over the years, but failing that, they're more than willing to settle for interchangeable stat machines.

You should have seen this coming, of course. Few free agent departures are a shock to those who keep close tabs

on the business end of football. A team will make overtures to sign any player of value to a long-term extension
long before his contract expires. If that offer isn't to the
player's liking, there will commence a great deal of sulking and holding out and everything else Terrell Owens
does twice a week.

So by the time the player does finally leave, the fans are
well prepared for it, having watched the player's final embittered season with the team, during which he put up big
stats but interacted with no one on the sidelines. Forewarn-
ing does not necessarily ease the sense of loss or betrayal.
Coping with loss is always a struggle, even when it was a
player you were kind of glad to see go, like DeAngelo Hall
or Rex Grossman. Grief can work itself out in familiar pat-
terns, and if you're prepared for them, it should really lessen
the blow of losing favor for that athlete you never met.

VIII.3.A THE FIVE STAGES OF FREE AGENT DEJECTION

1. **Run the Player's Name Through the Mud on the Internet**—Rant incessantly about what a clubhouse cancer
the guy was and how the team is prepared to skyrocket
to greatness without the burden of his negative presence. Lay out statistically tedious and unconvincing
arguments against him that no one wants to hear.
"Did you know his yard-per-catch average deceased
15 percent in 4 p.m. games played in the snow? An

unmistakable sign that he's soft if there ever was one! That reserve taking his place so should've had his job years ago anyway. So what if he only had twelve catches in four seasons!? Those were big-time snags. You wouldn't know unless you watched the team on a regular basis!"

2. Burn the Bum's Jersey—The most destructive, and therefore more cathartic, of the stages. Be sure to get good video of that puppy going up in flames and get it on YouTube, preferably with a death metal track as an overlay. Nothing else quite adds that vital touch of ridiculously tortured melancholy.

3. Blame Drew Rosenhaus—Even if the departing player isn't one of his clients. Like you need an excuse to hate on that slimy bag of goat afterbirth. Just don't let him know. He feeds his young with your regurgitated contempt like a mother bird.

4. Accept It—and for God's Sake, Do Not Continue Liking the Traitor on His New Team—That means you, Brett Favre and Joe Montana fans. *"But, but, he was real good for us for a long time! I'd follow him to the ends of the earth!! I can't turn my back on him now. In fact, I think I'll buy his jersey on the new team."* Die in a jersey bonfire. Team allegiance always supersedes your man-crush, unless you're part of his family. Even then it's dicey.

5. Get Ready to Shout Hateful Epithets Like You've Never Shouted Hateful Epithets Before When the Player Returns

to Play His Old, and Your Favorite, Team—You've been wronged and now's your chance for revenge. Boo that asshole like the greedy slut he is. Jeer him mercilessly for every mistake he commits, even to the point that you scare yourself. Maybe get some people in the crowd to help you tear apart an effigy of him. Eat a little of it for added effect. Nothing like the image of bloodthirsty mob violence to get in his head.

VIII.4 The Draft Is Excruciating, but in April You'll Take Anything You Can Get

An oasis in the bleak nothingness of April in the sports calendar, MLB Opening Day and the Masters be damned, the NFL Draft provides a weekend of NFL pseudo-activity that you can breathlessly follow. There are those who dismiss the draft as nothing more than a bland recitation of names, and maybe it is, but it's a recitation of names you'll soon be hearing during football games and that's about the best scrap you'll be thrown in the days of early spring.

Spread over two days, the draft really picks up steam after the seven-hour first round finally wraps up. It's also at that point that you'll find yourself completely in the dark about every player being taken. Not to worry, the NFL Draft drinking game is a time-honored tradition that will keep you entertained as grown men speak in glowing terms about the wonderful physical attributes of other grown men. A few wrinkles can be added any given year.

At the conclusion of the draft, in your supremely intoxicated state, you're all set to read through the draft grades assigned to each team by any of the dozens of self-described draft experts in the media. Each attempt at grading, of course, is prefaced by the handy reminder that there's no way of knowing the true value of a draft class for at least several years. If there's anything TV viewers want, it's an uninformed kneejerk reaction.

VIII.4.A THE NFL DRAFT DRINKING GAME

Mel Kiper Jr. petulantly objects to a team's selection because it doesn't jibe with his draft board.—Take one sip. How dare those teams defy him? Don't they know how meticulously he puts that board together? And how many players' agents he cozies up with to do it?

Chris Berman tips a pick to the television audience before it's announced by the commissioner.—Open every beer in the fridge and take the first sip out of the bottle. It's almost as obnoxious.

Jets fans boo one of their team's picks.—Take one sip. This will happen exactly as many times as the Jets have picks. Drink twice if they boo one of the Patriots' picks. Down a keg if they cheer for something.

A draftee cries or hugs the commissioner.— Pour one on the floor for his career.

A team selects the "best player available."—It

sounds redundant because surely teams should always be taking the best players, but this phrase is used to describe a team drafting a player who is the most talented rather than one who would fill a clear need on the roster.

A mention that a draftee's stock rose because of his play at the Senior Bowl.—Take two sips. The stellar Senior Bowl performance is a surefire springboard for a guy who gets taken way too high. Stupid NFL teams, when will they learn?

A draftee is filmed in the green room with friends and family.—One sip. Three if the player is being shown because he is falling down the draft order and now has a worried look on his face.

An analyst says of a draftee, "I love this guy's [*fill in the blank*]."—One sip if that thing is the player's intensity. Four if it's his plushie fetish.

Any of the following terms are used: "upside," "war room," "character issues," "motor," "reach," "need pick," "project," "intangibles," "combine."—One sip per use. Might need to keep a drink in each hand to keep up.

A player is complimented for "finishing plays."— Finish the drink in your hand.

A draftee is spotted wearing a yellow, purple, orange, or electric blue suit.—Take one sip if the player is black. Shotgun three beers if the player is white.

Each time Ed Werder reports from Dallas.—Make a

manly beer mustache on your face. A goatee if Jason Witten feeds him slander about a teammate.

A team lets its allotted time expire.—Drink an entire beer. If it's your team, drink a bucket of varnish. It's only happened a few times, most infamously in 2003 when the Vikings allowed the time to expire on the number seven pick of the draft, after which two teams rushed to pick in front of them. The Vikings fell to the ninth overall selection.

A mention of Tom Brady being the 199th player selected in the 2000 draft.—Take one sip. This will keep you going in the later rounds as pundits look for examples of second-day steals. This will invariably be the first one mentioned. And the first one repeated another ten times.

A player from the Ivy League is drafted.—Chug a bottle of 1943 vintage Château Latour. TV analysts, especially Chris Berman (he only occasionally makes mention of his years at Brown), adore it when one of the downtrodden denizens of the Ivy League gets a chance to shine in the NFL. Because those beleaguered souls never really get a fair shake in the world, do they?

The Lions select a receiver in the first round.—Take three sips. Sure, the Matt Millen era in Detroit has thankfully been swept into the dustbin of history (even if he returned to the broadcast table at NBC somehow). But that doesn't mean his successors aren't capable of repeating his mistakes. For the purposes of our enjoyment, let's hope they do.

A punter or a kicker is drafted.—Everyone knows you don't need to draft a kicker or a punter, not when any number of adequate ones will be available on the free agent market. Take two drinks if the punter drafted won the Ray Guy Award in college. Take three drinks if the pick is in the third round or higher. Then call your friend the Raiders fan to laugh at him.

The telecast cuts away to commercial on the second day of the draft before you have a chance to read your team's selections on the scroll.—Throw a bottle at the screen.

A montage of Mr. Irrelevants.—Drink whatever you got left. Looks like the draft is coming to a close. Mr. Irrelevant, the name attached to the final player selected in the draft because this player seldom even makes the team's final roster, has to be paraded around and embarrassed for not being a prized prospect. Still, it's better than not being taken at all. Those players are likely to be joining you on the couch, forty-ounce in hand, in a few months, if they're not being used as tackling dummies for a team's starters.

VIII.5 The Arena League and the CFL Are a Sickening Farce and Not Even the Good Kind of Sickening Farce

While nowhere near the embarrassment that was Vince McMahon's XFL—at the top of its litany of ills during its one-year existence was the resurrection of Tommy Maddox's career—the Arena Football League is an ongoing (well, maybe not) putrid blight upon the sporting landscape and, worse still, is responsible for Kurt Warner's emergence as an NFL signal caller. Russell Athletic ESPN Arena Football, as the longwinded official name of its broadcast goes, isn't so odious because arena football is any less watchable than baseball, hockey, or any of those other piddling games for pussybaskets. No, since Arena Football bears a tenuous similarity to the glorious game that gives us a good dose of nonsexual wood, its continued presence insults the NFL. At least its disparity in skill level does.

This is a league that features padded sidelines, rebound nets that the ball can bounce off of and still be in play, a four-point dropkick field goal, and players who are a dropped pass away from bagging groceries or, if they're lucky, playing a guy bagging groceries in a porn flick. It's no wonder that the league had to cancel its season this year due to economic woes.

Meanwhile, the minor league version of the Arena League is called af2, or arenafootball2, which is spelled out like a retarded teenager's message board commenter name. This is a league that boasts teams named the Oklahoma City Yard Dawgz, Quad City Steamwheelers (were the Quad City DJs too obvious a reference?), the Tri-Cities Fever (which, to its credit, does sound like a virulent strain of taint itch), and the Bossier-Shreveport

Battle Wings (which are very good in mambo sauce, I hear). This couldn't be any more of a Mickey Mouse operation if the league had advertisements on its sidelines. Oh, wait, it does. Mitsubishi has the naming rights to all the league's divisions, for marketing out loud! The funniest aspect of the Arena League shuttering for a season is that its independently run development league is continuing as planned. So, if you can't do without the palpable charge that comes from watching a glorified substitute for indoor soccer, treat yourself to the players who couldn't even qualify for that.

In the glaring absence of the indoor Nerfball league that is constantly plugged by ESPN (not surprising, considering the network's partial ownership stake in it), the all-too friendly Canucks will be glad to offer you a summertime dose of their bastardized version of the One True Sport. As one might expect, Canada makes a complete hash of it, giving you a joke of a league that has 110-yard playing fields and twelve players on each side going through three-down possessions. What's more, there are quotas in place to guarantee that each team maintains a certain minimum of Canadian players. Meaning there is a defined ceiling for how good any CFL team can be before it gets weighed down by the suckage of homegrown players unfit for local municipal hockey leagues.

Granted, the CFL has helped develop a handful of talented players and coaches for its immeasurably superior American counterpart, the most notable among them being Warren Moon, Doug Flutie, Marv Levy, and Joe Theismann. Nevertheless, any league that awards a point for a missed field goal or a punt out of the back of the opponent's end zone is possessed of a uselessness on par with Matt Leinart.

The latest emergent alternative for that football dollar is the United Football League, which is all but destined to fail like the USFL before it, even if Roger Goodell said he envisions the UFL eventually becoming a development league for the NFL. The league is officially scheduled to begin play in 2010, with an abbreviated inaugural season set for this fall, thus ensuring it gets buried behind the avalanche of NFL action. In a minor coup, the league has tapped former NFL coaches Dennis Green, Jim Haslett, and Jim Fassel, as well as former defensive coordinator Ted Cottrell, to helm its four teams. Undoubtedly, nothing stirs the masses like inferior talent led by once notable head coaches who've all squandered their fifth chance at success.

Fans would love nothing more than having the possibility of year-round football, but not at the price of a game with an over/under of 700 points and a quality of play even lower than a Week 17 Chiefs-Rams tilt (but without the added entertainment of recalcitrant players taking plays off and openly flouting coaches). In the end, the worst of the NFL far outstrips even the height of what the Arena League and the CFL have to offer. Let's not kid ourselves with these cheap imitations. As everybody knows, an arena is for Judas Priest concerts, a stadium is for football. And Canada is for the poutine-stained denim jacket-and-jeans combo. We should keep it that way.

VIII.6 Beware the Post–NBA Finals Misery Vortex

Of the desolate voids that typify the ungodly horror that is the off-season, none is worse than the month that lurches from the end of the NBA Finals in mid-June until the NFL teams report to training camp in the third week of July. There you will find nothingness. Then more nothingness. Then some sunny nothingness. Then some goddamn baseball, followed soon after by another unbroken stretch of nil.

Sure, post–Super Bowl February is plenty dreadful, but at least the buzz from the recently concluded season hasn't entirely subsided. Plus there are still coaches and GMs being hired and fired, which is a delight in and of itself. And, hey, March Madness is right around the corner, which is actually kinda-sorta fun for the first two rounds, until you lose your office pool to a girl who picks the Final Four based on where she applied to grad school. In the following months you get a little caught up with playoff hockey and basketball. You even go to MLB Opening Day and decide it's a little charming, but still don't watch more than three innings of baseball until September.

By then, the thought that you might just tough out this off-season is winning out. That is, until you hit the early summer wall and are staring down the biggest lacuna in the sports calendar. NFL news, if there's any at all, is scant. The only goddamn sport to watch is baseball. Summer movies are out but two-thirds of them are piss-poor comic book adaptations and assorted retreads.

The best you can hope for is a scandal on the scale of the Michael Vick fiasco to crop up, but those only come along once every so often. Granted, there's typically one decent scandal per off-season, but that was a particularly good one. When they're bad, they're Favre-speculation-about-unretiring bad.

Every football fan struggles during this stretch, but it's incumbent upon you to forge through the abyss with your sanity intact. Heading to the beach for several weeks and getting really blotto will not only help the time fly by but will give you the rare exposure to the sun that you're usually robbed of by spending months in a bar. Conserving your vacation time so you can attend training camp? Throw yourself into your work. The sudden uptick in production may offset the dozens of days you took off because you were hungover the year before.

Enough time goes by and, then, one magnificent morn, you switch on your television and, hark, what delightful sound strikes your ear? News of a holdout? JaMarcus Russell won't be reporting to camp next week because of a contract dispute. Truly this marks the first sign of a rebirth, of a season starting anew.

Yes.

It begins!

8.7 Training Camp Is Miserable for the Athlete, Only Kind of Boring for You

Without exception, NFL players loathe training camp. For them it's an endless procession of rote drills and grueling two-a-days cruelly imposed by taskmaster coaches. It's where players who report 30 pounds overweight from the off-season bust their asses for a few weeks only to possibly not even make final cut. As Redskins tight end/H-back Chris Cooley put it so eloquently in a post on the toweringly sexy football humor blog Kissing Suzy Kolber:

> The one cool thing about the first month of camp is living in a dorm room. I love it when I get to leave my 2.8 million dollar house and live in a 400 square foot box, trade in the Mercedes for the bus, and curl up in my twin bed. The TV's are great too, who isn't happy when they pick up 10 total channels on a 24 inch box? Yeah, I guess now people can say what a ungrateful bastard I am and how much anyone would give to play pro football, but please, whether it's a high school or NFL training camp, it's still gonna be as fun as a bag of dicks.

This unmitigated suffering is one reason why training camp should be appealing to the fan. Seeing incredibly wealthy people shunted into meager living conditions and put through the wringer in any other context would be a wonderful concept for a reality show, one that you would gladly tune into each and every week. And certainly more tolerable than the ones Michael Irvin and T.O. have. That the millionaires in question are physically able to handle the rigors should only diminish the allure slightly.

Into the whole awkward adulation thing? There's plenty of that too. Take the opportunity to shake players' hands and exchange a few lines of stilted conversation. Well, at least that's how it was back in the era when every team held camps open to the public. Nowadays, fewer than half the teams in the league hold training camps that are publicly accessible. Most have repaired to the antiseptic confines of team facilities, where coaches can berate players and run all the obscure situational bullshit they'll never use in the regular season in complete seclusion. Which means you just know they're all having coke-and-hookers parties after every practice. Quit hogging it all for yourself, NFL teams.

For all the tedium, there are still some folksy charming sights at training camp. For one, there are the players you know have no shot at making the roster. Look at them toil futilely. Let them know in advance how you'd like your groceries bagged and on which side of the doorstep to leave your FedEx deliveries. They'll appreciate the heads-up.

Then there are moments of Norman Rockwell–like Americana that infuse the experience with something other than the corporate culture that has come to pervade the NFL experience at every level. The Packers, for example, have players who ride children's bikes pre- and post-practice with the kids riding on the handlebars. All right, that's really the last vestige of hands-on down-home whimsy to be found at any of these glorified practices. Still, by the outset of summer, you've undergone what's already been a six-month separation from your favorite team. By now, you'd sit in ninety-five degree heat just to watch them stand around and text their friends.

VIII.8 Observe *Madden* Day Like the National Holiday It Should Be

For the past twenty-plus years, video game publisher Electronic Arts Tiburon has brought gamers and football fans (these two categories have a bit of overlap) the premier console football simulator on the market. Of course, ever since EA was granted the exclusive NFL license in 2004, it's the only one on the market, but y'know, details, details. What do you need competition for? Granting monopolies to large corporations is what America does best.

The game is named for the Hall of Fame coach and occasionally coherent grumbling recently retired broadcaster John Madden, who, in a way, is to video games what George Foreman is to electric grills: a sports celebrity who haphazardly picked something to which to attach his name. However, beginning last year, Madden stopped recording play-by-play audio for the game, thus reducing the number of times you'll hear "Boom!" during game play by roughly 100 percent. He was replaced by the duo of Tom Hammond and Cris Collinsworth, who have the collective personality of a Tim Robbins beer fart.

Each August, a teeming unwashed horde of single guys in authentic Mitchell & Ness jerseys queue up by the hundreds at the local Gamestop the night of the release to drop sixty dollars on a game that is little more than the previous year's edition plus a roster update and a few new player animations. Yeah, I know. I love it too.

It's a joyous occasion for no other reason than that it's another signal, along with the arrival of training camp and the preseason, that the blessed NFL regular season is drawing near. When you've had to endure nothing but months of baseball, you'll lap up anything resembling football like it's mother's milk. What's more, you can play through an entire season with your favorite team before the actual season begins. You can tell yourself it's your way of scouting the competition. Did you get the Eagles to finish 19-0 and win the Super Bowl 49–3? On the easiest difficulty setting? Well, surely that's how it's going to shake out in real life.

Unfortunately for we socially deficient freaks, this release falls on a Tuesday, smack in the middle of a work week. Just as the government denies fans a vacation day after the Super Bowl, our rights are trampled on with the refusal of time off for *Madden* Day. Now the drill goes: you get the game at midnight, only so you can go back home and hit the sack before work the next day? Maybe at best you can fit in a game or two, but that's it. Oh, nononono, my friends. That be some bullshit. Not only have you waited through a seemingly endless off-season, but also a couple hours of standing around in a sausage-fest in order to get this game, and now you can't even play it? If you're going to go to that much effort to procure *Madden*, you need to have a *Madden* Day Plan in place.

Because *Madden* sells approximately eleventy-seven trillion copies a year, many employers have now cottoned onto the fact that a metric shitload of people attempt to take off the day the game comes out and have implemented policies forbidding workers from using vacation on that date. Why? Because they're rank assholes and assholes love nothing more than throwing around whatever meager power they have at their disposal. If you happen to be one of those supervisor humps, congrats. You can take the day off and leave the outraged underlings to choke on your hypocrisy. That was easy, huh?

For the rest of us, there are a number of options available. The simplest solution, of course, is to quit your job. Sure, slogging through med school was arduous and extremely expensive, but not letting you take a day off to play a video game just because you have a surgery scheduled is a crock. Besides, as a surgeon you're already predisposed with the precise hand-eye coordination necessary to excel at *Madden*. All that remains is the capacity to yell sophomoric insults over a headset.

Having some foresight can be to your benefit. It's probably unlikely that a relative will have the courtesy to die around the release of *Madden*, which would give you an easy out. However, if one should pass away earlier in the year, say around April, prevail upon your family to consider the merits of a summer burial. The soil is less barren and there are more bugs to expediate decomposition. Stick the corpse on ice for a few months and convince the relatives it's a farewell tour.

Whatever you do, don't try to feign an illness. Most bosses reflexively won't buy it, whether you're actually sick or not, and will demand some sort of doctor's note, and depending on your financial situation, a doctor's visit might be a lot to sacrifice for a single day of gaming. Contracting a really serious illness in advance to seal the deal is an extra step worthy of admiration and a surefire way to score some playing time. The nurses can probably rig the game up on your hospital TV. If you can time your eventual passing with the clinching of a Super Bowl victory, you can go out a champion, and perhaps bequeath your screen name to a close relative. That is, until the coroner overwrites the file on your memory card hours later with an 8-8 season with the Chiefs. What a dick.

One thing to keep in mind once you fabricate an excuse valid-sounding enough to get the day off is that you shouldn't load any *Madden* highlights you may have that day onto YouTube, not only because it's an asinine practice in general, but because the time stamp on the videos will give away your ruse. Ridiculous as it sounds, you'd be surprised how Internet savvy employers have become.

Also, learning the profile name of the boss's kid before-hand is a must. The last thing you want is to be playing some thirteen-year-old on Xbox Live and let it slip that you're skipping work from your teller job at the bank just for the kid to recognize your name from one of his dad's endless rants about work.

No matter how you go about securing yourself some glorious playing time with *Madden*, keep in mind that if you ever play the game using any team other than the one you root for in real life, you're a gutless traitor fit for castration by a scythe. I don't care if the Saints do only have a 75 rating in the game. If you play with the Patriots, even to beat a clearly superior opponent, you've lowered yourself to such an extent that even the most cogent of excuses cannot explain away your fanhood cowardice. Unless you have money on the game. That's something anyone can understand.

VIII.9 Dupe Yourself into Thinking the Preseason Matters

It's a well-known but somehow little-acknowledged fact that the NFL preseason is an empty spectacle possessed of a meaninglessness that exists only on par with award shows and philosophy classes. However, after six agonizing months of football deprivation you'd stick your dick in a hornet's nest to get anything resembling the game you so sickeningly crave. And NFL teams know that. That's why it's a perfect opportunity for them to fleece fans with exorbitant prices for what amounts to maybe a quarter of actual football (if that).

In the best of circumstances, preseason games are where closely contested arcane position battles are settled (the battle for third-string tight end is on!). It's also where a team decides whether or not to carry a fourth safety or a seventh linebacker on the final roster. Truly riveting stuff, I know. For everyone on the field whose job isn't on the line, it's a tedious dress rehearsal where coaches try not to reveal too much of their playbook and the main goal for players is not to get hurt. Donovan McNabb, especially, likes to save his injuries for the regular season.

But knowing it means nothing to the players themselves, how then can the preseason be more exciting for you? Yes, there's beer. And whiskey. And tequila. And vodka. And paint thinner. All these intoxicants will be necessary in surviving this stolid ordeal. Just remind yourself that consequential football is drawing near. Drawing from your powers of extreme self-delusion, you'll make it through this thing yet. Delude yourself enough and you might even learn to enjoy it in a Stockholm syndrome kind of way. Because, after all, in preseason games either team's starters play anywhere between one drive and little over one half of the game. That's a lot of empty time to fill with guys who are getting cut in a week. Your psychosis might as well pick up the slack.

Watching at home, this is no biggie. You could simply change the channel. Then again, it's the summer, so nothing is on except baseball and second-rate shows networks haul out for the dry months. But that's irrelevant. You're a real fan, one of the true believers who forked over fifty dollars (plus fifteen for parking) to see your favorite team take the field in a meaningless scrimmage. Because your season ticket package required you to. That expense has to be justified. Here's where the self-delusion comes in handy.

As with any destructive habit, you must give yourself to it completely. In many ways, like the players, you too should approach the preseason as a dress rehearsal. Except, unlike those players, you should care. A lot. Like Ron Paul supporters a lot. Whipping yourself into a frenzy for the regular season isn't a switch you can just flip on and off. Weeks of building up alcohol tolerance and ascertaining the best routes for eluding security will give you an edge many lesser fans will lack, thus landing them either passed out or in jail.

Having readied yourself for spectator misbehavior, you must now work your expectations for your team's upcoming season into a fine, ranch-flavored froth. This means outrageous, even wholly insane pipe dreams with no basis in reason and without regard to past performance. Redskins fans have perfected this art. Because of the parity that has come through free agency and the salary cap, teams can swing between being dominant and dominated from year to year. For the majority of teams in the league (everybody except the Lions) there exist some faint glimmer of hope that this can be the year when it all comes together for a title run. Just look at the Falcons and Dolphins in 2008. And nowhere are those delusions stoked more pathologically than during the preseason. Massage that faint glimmer until it become a powerful klieg light blinding to anyone foolish enough to question your team's chances.

With so little exposure to the players that will be carrying the team throughout the regular season, every iota of playing time in the preseason must be overexamined and treated as though it's indicative of the entire year to come. Did the starting quarterback go 5-for-5 with a touchdown in his only drive? FUCK YEAH! EMM VEE PEE! SUPER BOWL YEAR, BAY-BEE! Did the starting running back average under four yards a carry in his two touches? Wonder how he feels about a severed pig's head in his mailbox? Similarly, the preseason can be a minefield for spiking the fantasy football value of some minor-role players, who end up racking up insane numbers against third-string defenses, only to return to being regular old Kevin Jones in the regular season. Don't be fooled by these preseason stalwarts.

The presence of irrelevant players is no reason to stop caring about the outcome of the game, either. Just because your team was ahead 13–10 when the starters got pulled doesn't mean victory has been attained. Do you want them to finish with a losing record in the preseason? That's just the kind of weak momentum that can carry over into the regular season, dooming what would have surely been a memorable title run. Yes. That's more like it. Scream your lungs out at the sparsely filled stadium. You've already started to care about these meaningless second-half scrubs, haven't you? So begins the descent into the fan madness.

After each contest, be sure to call in to local radio shows to express your overzealous observations of these pointless affairs. It may not seem so, but coaches regularly tune in to these programs before making important roster moves and playbook alternations. Generally they only heed the loudest, most deranged testimonials, so keep that in mind if you get on the air.

ARTICLE IX

Taking Fandom to Unhealthy Levels—Then a Little Further

IX.1: Fandom on the Intarwebz!!11!

Finding that your manic pleas for the fullback to get a few more touches per game have fallen on deaf ears? You've tried writing four-page profanity-laced screeds to the local newspaper columnist. You've kidnapped the pets of the area sports radio call-in show. You've yelled vehemently at anyone on the street wearing your team's colors. You've run cars off the road bearing a team logo bumper sticker, then proceeded to berate and frighten the driver as he reaches for a cell phone to call the cops. In a final fit of pique, you even stood outside the team's headquarters dressed in animal pelts with a bullhorn and poorly edited signage. What's a monomaniacal true football fan to do?

Lucky for you, you live in the age of the Internet, which was created primarily to give people with singular obsessions and foot fetishes a venue in which their vices can fester and grow larger from finding other like-minded and

like-perverted freaks, most of whom have the spelling ability of Terry Bradshaw. Utilizing this wondrous medium,
you can air your views on any and all subjects, no matter
how ill-informed and laden with obscure *Simpsons* ref-
erences your commentary, to an audience of potentially
dozens. From now on, no one will be able to ignore your
calls to bench the starting quarterback after Week 2 or
trade for a star receiver, even though the team has neither
the trade collateral nor the cap room. That's the beauty
of it. Anything goes! Even the asinine. Even gratuitous
pictures of cheerleaders. Especially gratuitous pictures of
cheerleaders!

Despite what clueless old dipshits like Michael Wilbon
will tell you, the Internet is not a monolithic entity. There
are, in fact, a very large swath of worthless places for you
to visit online while being unproductive at work.

Mainstream Media Sites

The MSM presence online is largely composed of reprinted
content that originally appeared in your daily newspaper,
weekly newsmagazine, or up-to-the-second cable news
network broadcast, most of which is just rewritten Associated Press stories. The material typically strives to
be balanced and dispassionate, though it favors the East
Coast, liberal values, Disney's financial interests, scrappy
(white) players, and athletes who don't reflexively hate
reporters. Because its sports coverage depends greatly on
the privileged access to athletes and league officials that

media professionals can't afford to lose, the MSM tone is by nature antiseptic and inoffensive, and therefore painfully, painfully boring.

In terms of utility to the modern fan, these are good places to get immediate news alerts, scores, the recap of a game you already saw the highlights from seven hours ago, injury reports, and canned quotes from stars. Keenly sensing their own obsolescence, many MSM outlets have tried to incorporate elements of new media, such as blogs and comment sections (which are mysteriously closed for some more high-profile writers), into their sites. However, as these features are subject to the same standards of decency as their parent companies—no swearing, no overt misogyny, no trash-talk, no threatening statements—they are of little use to actual fans.

Message Boards

Message boards are visually Spartan and aggressively unedited forums where groups of anonymous mouth-breathers bandy petty insults, usually in a tone marked by misanthropy, profanity, and casual racism (though not in the excusably clever way sports satirists employ these ills to hilarious effect). All this putative discussion is done in the context of discussing a subject in the news. Message board commenters are of the opinion that the Internet peaked with the advent of the Drudge Report's siren GIFs.

As a rule, the titular subject in any message board thread is discussed rationally for an average duration of two or three comments, at which point it veers wildly off course as someone's mom is compared to Hitler and chaos breaks out in a flurry of LOLspeak and run-on insults. Of course, the first casualties of any Internet flame war are proper syntax and the ability to make moderate use of capital letters. JUST LIKE THIS! DOESN'T IT MAKE MY WORDS SEEM STENTORIAN AND DIM-WITTED AT THE SAME TIME? Someone will spell "bitch" with a percentage sign. Don't be alarmed. That's just sort of how it goes on messages boards.

Though the level of discourse contained within message boards hovers somewhere around "shit you'll hear in a mall Lids store," these forums offer the closest approximation of the drunken trash-talking that goes on during tailgating most Sundays. The difference being that, while it's an often innocent and amusing way of provoking knife fights in the parking lot, it's suddenly unbelievably dorky when you do it on the Net.

Blogs

Though MSM writers continue to propagate the threadbare, wildly inaccurate stereotype that bloggers are unemployed losers sitting in their parents' basements pissing away their pathetic lives spreading unsubstantiated rumors about public figures, most bloggers actually work in their parents' living room, thus granting themselves easier access to the kitchen and its multitudes of Supreme Pizza Hot Pockets and Shasta Cola. Successful blogs, by and large, combine the qualities of mainstream media sites and message boards in a crude, tantalizing admixture that requires of their authors shrewd news judgment, a lapidary wit, a taste for vulgarity, and deep cache of Erin Andrews pictures.

Unlike message boards, with their armies of subliterate posters, blogs are typically written by an individual or a small group of authors who are for the most part capable of stringing together complete sentences, if not always coherent thoughts. The writing style is often lazily referred to as snarky, though it has yet to be proven that the fictional snark created by Lewis Carroll ever wrote for a Gawker site. Often, authors of blogs have at least some minor background in writing (composing fake Craigslist ads does count as writing experience), a boring office job, a boring spouse, and lofty career goals they would strive toward if only they weren't spending the time blogging.

Blogs can be many different things, all of them as frightening to Bob Costas as the ghastly practice of gambling on sports. The route a blog can go is entirely up to the author. It can be something as basic and innocent as a personal diary (of sex), a journal of someone's vacation (sex cruise), or even quick ruminations on topics of the day (sex advice). Accordingly, they can be broadly thematic, narrowly focused, or just a collection of images of awkward-looking people with superimposed LOLCats-inspired captions. With eleventy million blogs forming every hour, you have to do something to be distinctive and build a readership. That way, you feel like people are tuning in for your views, when really they want to jerk it to the Keeley Hazell photo you posted. Either way, the delusion is intoxicating.

An important lesson to remember when trying to establish yourself in the blogosphere is to befriend your fellow bloggers. They can assist with driving traffic to your site, promoting your blog, helping you refine your voice, and offering interesting content to steal. Remember, though, that if you comment on a news story or a viral video you have to credit whichever blog had it first, even if the subject is a news story posted on ESPN.com that a million people will read whether or not blogs write about it. It's an incredibly lame practice, but you must abide by this item of blog decorum or an disturbing lifelike effigy of you will be burned in *Second Life*.

Once you're ready to begin, you can use any number of free blogging programs to get up and running. Try to give it a clever name, preferably something that pokes fun at Travis Henry's penchant for unprotected sex (at press time, he's sired eleven kids by ten different woman). Or, failing that, something randomly vulgar. Might I recommend Cris Collinsworth's Appalling Girth?

If your soul-crushing, non-football-related job places you in an organization run by humorless tightasses, like, say, the *Washington Post*, you will need to adopt a blogging pseudonym, lest your boss Google your real name, discover your ramblings, and take issue with the post where you called Mark Sanchez a cockharvester seven hundred times in three paragraphs. But what should you call yourself in the blogosphere? There are no ironclad rules, though this is the rare case where something homerific like bearsfn6832 probably won't hack it. (Unless you're a woman, then feel free to call yourself something perfectly insipid like Diamondbacks Chick. Sure, it's a lazy name, but it sends an unmistakable message to the preponderence of single men in the blogosphere that you are receptive to their awkward overtures.) People respect something funny and eye-catching. Or at least an *Arrested Development* reference. Failing that, just be extraordinarily crude and cruel. To bloggers, they're the same thing!

If you stick with the blogging game long enough, eventually advertisers will offer you piddling sums to place banner ads that cover half the top page of your blog. And you'll take it without thinking twice. Because that sum, however miniscule, represents money you made being a fan. And though that amount is far outstripped by the value of the hundreds of hours you spent blogging when you could have been trying to get your masters, it offers a handy excuse to loved ones who allege your blogging is useless. "No," you'll say, shoving into their faces the $112 check that represents three months of revenue from the site. "This be a cash-flow machine, motherfucker."

IX.2: Heed the Officially Licensed Section on NFL Apparel and Merchandise

To fully live the football dream, you must make yourself a walking billboard for your team by covering yourself and your meager possessions in branded gear. Whether that means team bumper stickers dotting your car, sporting teamware head-to-toe, or team-colored tackling dummies in your yard, no one will ever mistake you for a person of rounded interests. Or, worse still, a follower of a rival team.

NFL teams have succeeded in merchandizing every conceivable consumer product on the market, and even a few of the basic elements of the universe. If you look at the periodic table, you'll notice that the *G* in the *Ga* representing gallium is really the Packers' logo. Be advised to keep it away from the Bears' logo in cerium.

This army of products is mostly stocked with items lacking in even the most tenuous relation to the sport itself. In most cases, they come in the form of regular household objects like, say, vacuum cleaner bags, a GPS machine, or an inhaler. Naturally, it's your duty as a fan to fill your home to the point of overflow with these team-themed gadgets. If the team alters its logo or color scheme, unload half of it. Gotta stay current with some of your possessions. The rest maintains your vintage credentials. Sure, usually such changes are a transparent attempt by the team to churn up some quick revenue, but are you really going to deny them that? Without the cash influx, they might not be able to stay competitive! They'll be forced to sign second-tier free agents. Your team might even end up with Gus Frerotte!

If you follow the trademark rules of the NFL, only officially licensed goods are approved for purchase, but no one without a luxury box has the dispensable income to invest in that much overpriced love. Fortunately, all manner of chintzy crap (sorry, beautiful and imaginative crap) with your team's logo on it can be found at craft fairs, yard sales, or from shady merchants outside the stadium on gameday. Just because it was made with without a trademark hologram sticker doesn't mean it wasn't made with love.

For the handyman, the fun doesn't stop. In 2006, Home Depot and Glidden began offering a line of team paints that exactly matched the colors of every franchise in the league. Now you can rest easy knowing that the color of your walls and the pants of a bunch of dudes you cheer on once a week are in perfect aesthetic harmony. Now, if you could only find team hair dye to match that of the starting quarterback, you'd be all set. Just kidding. That would be deeply unsettling. I mean, except when *you* do it.

Your house, your person, your pets: It's all a blank, beautiful canvas stretching out before you, begging to be splayed over with merch. Look at the options before you for personal adornment: hats, wacky glasses, earrings, watches, shirts, jerseys, wristbands, helmets, foam fingers, hoodies, Mardi Gras beads, socks, sweatpants, belt buckles, fanny packs, concealable bludgeons for beating people with fanny packs, wigs, condoms, prescription soles, hearing aids, license-plate frames, gangsta grills, cock rings, nipple clamps, creepy contact lenses, home pregnancy tests, and ties for your dad. The possibilities are only constrained by your imagination. And the extent to which you have access to drugs potent enough to make you buy this much stuff.

Of all the fan accessories out there, Fatheads are an especially curious case. They are life-size stickers of players that are intended to be placed on your wall. Now, I understand player adulation as well as the next fan, but having a realistic likeness of a guy on your wall, regardless of how great a player he is, is about a step away of having a blow-up doll of him. You might as well go the whole hog at that point.

NFL teams are helpful in that they enjoy shaping your consuming habits for you. Enterprising retailers can enter into sponsorship agreements with teams to have themselves designated the official something or other of an NFL team. For example, Harris Teeter is the official grocery store of the Washington Redskins and the Carolina Panthers (two-timers!). That way, if you're a Redskins or a Panthers fan and you purchase your frozen pizzas or toilet paper from another store, it's like you're aiding and abetting the enemy. I hope that TP you got chafes your asshole, traitor.

If all that's not enough, there are always credit card companies that offer team-themed cards with predatory interest rates. Yes, indeed: the reputation of sports fans is that of being so blindly devoted that they'll enter into any deal, no matter how inane, so long as the team's logo appears somewhere on the object of their fleecing.

But it's not always about the league exploiting your poor fiscal decisions. On occasion, you can make good on the poor economic straits of players themselves. On more than a few occasions, players from Super Bowl–winning teams of the distant past will auction off their championship rings on eBay. Last year, Larry Brown sold off one of his three rings he won with the Cowboys. A fan who leans toward the aristocratic could parade one of these around, not only affirming his fan cred, but the weaknesses of the player pension system. Double score!

The most contentious debate in apparel etiquette centers on the thorny issue of jersey wear. This rift, if left unresolved, threatens to tear all of fandom asunder. The majority of people attending games find the jersey a perfectly acceptable expression of fandom. However, a rogue band of contrarians insist that the notion of wearing jerseys, replica or authentic, is ridiculous on its face. "What, you think if the team is a man down they're gonna call you down from the stands?" they chide. Hey, it could happen!

What these tight-assed prigs of the pigskin don't understand is that jerseys are a vital, if, yes, somewhat silly way for fans to connect with the game they'll never be a part of. Because football pants are otherworldly ugly and helmets obscure vision (though they're helpful when bottles are being thrown at you by Jets fans), the jersey is the most sensible part of the uniform to wear in a casual setting. So scorn away, you aloof bunch of judgmental taintstabbers.

You're the type of people who take all the fun out of life, like nosy cops and neighbors who can't take a little celebratory gunfire after a win.

Customized name jerseys, however, are another matter entirely. People who wear personalized NFL jerseys with their own last name on the back are an affront to God and deserve to die in a landslide. Your own name only serves to remind other fans how tragically distant you are from the action. If you are going to customize the name on a jersey, at least have the decency to do it in a way that amuses other people. Unfortunately, the NFL does you no favors in this regard, as the league keeps an extensive list of banned words that can't be put on a jersey ordered from NFL Shop. When it was revealed years back that former dogfight impresario and quarterback Michael Vick went by the pseudonym Ron Mexico when dealing with a woman who later alleged that he infected her with herpes, fans tried to order customized number 7 Falcons jerseys, but were immediately rejected. Because the league is full of humorless titblisters.

Another frequently spotted abomination is the fan who wears a jersey of a player who is no longer with the team. The only instances when this is acceptable are if said player is a retired star or the player is a longtime fan favorite (at least seven years of service!) with your team who has only left to play out his final few unproductive seasons on a non-contending team. Otherwise, you might as well be proclaiming yourself a fair-weather fan who hasn't shown interest in rooting for the team in years. You don't want to be left out when fellow fans are passing out shots, after all.

IX.3: Dress Your Pet, Because They Can't Tell You It's Lame

If you had to identify which sports fan base is the most likely to have its followers dress up pets in ridiculous themed outfits, you'd probably guess NASCAR fans. But NFL fans wouldn't be that far off. Yes, obsession over football is indeed a virulent pathology, one that carries over to everything within sight, animal or car bumper. And there's nothing a pet-owning sports fan loves more than annoying and possibly terrifying their dearest animal companions by forcibly covering the poor beast in a hand-sewn Giants sweater.

The sad fact remains that thirty-one NFL teams prohibit the admission of any non-seeing-eye animal to their stadium. St. Louis' policy, however, remains open to goats, though in recent years it has been limited to those with a documented living arrangement with a human. That means, mostly likely, your Vietnamese potbelly pig is staying at home during the big game. Which is a shame, because they'd probably totally get a kick out of an environment where the people are the ones acting like braying animals.

Clothing isn't the be-all, end-all of pet humiliation, however. There's still the matter of naming the poor buggers. Mainstream society, misguided though it may be, frowns on bestowing upon your human children sports-related names, ruling out the possibility of a Dolphin4Life or Patsfan 1 for them. You'll just have to settle with giving them some boring mundane moniker like Joshua or a weird spelling of Jeremy (Jerheme Urban being the offspring of one such couple).

Pets, on the other hand: You can go batshit crazy with them. Hell, that's the point. Call the thing Purrless Price, Biletnikoff the Dog, or Lil' Rocky Bleier if you're so inclined. Whatever charges your phone.

Not all pets are created equal. Each demands its own specifically discomfiting costume or theme forced upon it.

Fish—Fish add a cool, almost sensual presence to any room. Some people even consider them seductive. And in spite of what you've been led to believe, fish are surprisingly good companions. However, fish, it should be said, make horrible football fans. You can't dress them in anything! You can't color the water in the tank to correspond with the team's or you'll kill the little scaled shits. The best you can do is get a little decorative scuba man with the team's logo on it. That's it. Fuck fish. They're not team players.

Ferret/Lizard/Spider/Ant Farm—Who owns these? They're the pets of contrarians and contrarians have no place in football. They should belong on the writing staff of Slate, which coincidentally has no business writing about the NFL. But that doesn't stop them from churning out mind-curdling pieces on why the loss of the force-out rule is actually good for receivers. In other words, screw these pets.

Snake—Giving the mice you feed them the name of the next opposing quarterback the team faces is a nice touch.

Turtle—The lesson of *Entourage*, other than that it became unwatchable after its second season, is that turtles love rare sneakers, ornately designed Yankees hats, and unkempt goatees. This makes them sympathetic to baseball douches and therefore unsuitable to football fandom.

Horse—If you're wealthy enough to own a horse, you can probably buy a team. Make sure to save a luxury suite for me, you rich asshole.

Dog—Well, for starters, you should probably eschew starving them, beating them, and breeding them to fight one another to the death. Glad we had this talk, Michael Vick from the year 2006.

Cat—The NFL is a league that generally appeals more to dog owners than to insular cat people, though that won't stand in the way of crazy cat ladies, who will collect enough cats to fill a fifty-three-feline roster of her own, replete with uniforms.

Bird—Taking into consideration the fact that birds aren't particular fearsome, there sure are a lot of teams named after them. That bird better be something imposing, like a falcon or other predatory bird, and that falconer's glove better be in team colors. Unless you like the Falcons, then it's kind of self-explanatory.

Monkey—Echoing the point from the previous item, somehow there are five goddamn lame-ass bird teams in the NFL and yet not a one named for a monkey. Knotty racial connotations might have something to do with it, but that doesn't stop the Redskins from hanging around. You and your monkey should protest the league office. If the project doesn't work out, he can still bring you beers. Just make sure he doesn't open them first. You don't wanna know what surprises he'll have waiting for you.

IX.4: The Mystery of Trash-Talking

Fandom, at least in the ideal, consists of more than simply showing up every week to the stadium, to the bar, or to the couch blanketed in team apparel and getting shitfaced. No, with great intoxication comes great belligerence. You've got to put that animosity to good use. But because swinging an awl to an opposing fan's faceplate is an arrestable offense in most states, you've got to do your damage with your words. Nasty blunt instruments of locution that devastate an enemy fan's will to live, or at least invokes his will to chuck a brick at you. Eliciting either response means you've gotten under his skin.

Trash-talk, like any martial art, must be executed with extreme discipline and well-honed precision. Solely screaming, "FUCK YOU, COWGIRLS FAN, YOU'RE A FUCKIN' LOOOOOOOSER! I HOPE TONY HOMO BREAKS HIS HURT PINKIE OFF IN YOUR BUTT-HOLE!" accomplishes nothing but to reflect poorly on you. Except that Romo line. That one was all right. Effectively unnerving comments go past the generic and get at something personal. And because fans don't care much for their own lives, that means you must mine the personal lives of the players for caustic remarks.

Calling Plaxico Burress "Plexiglas" inflicts little damage when compared to riffing on the reports of numerous police calls to his home regarding domestic abuse. Perhaps a better substitute is "Smacksaho Her-ass?" Preferably said while aiming gun-fingers at your thigh. Everyone who's seen an Eagles game knows Andy Reid is a free-floating planetary mass that draws McRibs into his gravitational field. But he's also a horribly inept parent. Be sure to identify any Eagles fans being arrested on game-day as either Garrett or Britt. Santonio Holmes got busted for marijuana possession, but he also exhibited his penis on the Internet. Commence cheers for the Santonio Dong Rodeo whenever you see a Steelers fan sporting his jersey. Marshawn Lynch boasts of his Beast Mode persona when in front of a microphone, but behind the wheel of a car he is a hit-and-run-machine. Therefore, running down Bills fans doubles as social commentary.

Because so much of trash-talking is based on how teams are faring at the point of their contest, their head-to-head histories, the rap sheets of their players, and how bumpkin-like their fan bases are, it's impossible to predict how any one team should approach verbally tearing down another. The best way to zero in on what riles the enemy is to listen to them, observe their fan message boards to find out what they dislike about their own team. Then hammer on them like Larry Fitzgerald on the mother of his children.

Before proceeding with reckless invective, there are several incontrovertible laws of the smack of which to be aware.

IX.4.A THE LAWS OF TRASH-TALKING

1. **To every perceived slight to a team there is an equal, or more likely excessive, countervailing blow.** Essentially, this falls squarely under the "don't start no shit won't be no shit" principle. Let not a foul word about another's team escape your lips lest you be prepared for things to get out of hand. Beer bottles, for instance. They get out of people's hands in a hurry.

2. **A fan who pleas for civility or tries to rat out a trash-talker to security is to be counted among the snitches. And, as the saying goes, they are to receive stitches.** Anyone who attends an NFL game expecting a polite, deferential atmosphere is, at best, mistaken, and, at worst, developmentally disabled. Have a thick skin or stay home. And don't try to hide behind your kids, saying you expected it was an atmo-

sphere friendly to their virgin ears. Horseshit. Don't try
to impose your rigid morals on football fans. I'm sure
there's something great on ABC Family right now if you
can't take it.

3. **When in doubt, always resort to the number of
   championships your team has won.** (Unless your
   team has won fewer titles than your enemy's, in which
   case resort to childish name-calling.)

4. **When your team is impossibly ahead, the world of
   trash-talking is your oyster.** Here's where the playbook really opens up. The morally righteous will tell
   you there are such things as bad winners. And they're
   right. That's the winner who doesn't bathe in his opponent's misery like a pig in shit. Rub your nipples whilst
   taunting the losers. Let them know you're really getting
   into it.

5. **When your team is ahead, but the outcome is still in
   doubt, be ever mindful of the forces of karma. The
   mood is good, no doubt, if still a little uneasy.** The
   last thing you want to do is start shooting your mouth
   off so much that you jinx the team. Then you'll not only
   have gloating enemy fans to listen to but the scornful
   eyes of friendly forces. Remind the opposition of the
   scoreboard, but don't act like it's a done deal. Someone
   might make a clever GIF image of you pointing smugly
   to the camera like Jeremy Shockey, just before failure
   descends.

6. **Should the game be tied, allow your concentrated hate to be the difference-maker.** Anxiety runs highest when things are tightly contested. This is when the team needs you most in the verbal war that doesn't affect the action on the field. Scream rivulets of obscenities that would make the hair of the worst Tourette's case stand on end. For reference, check out Chris Berman cutting room floor footage on YouTube.

7. **Your team is trailing, but there is still hope. Okay, there isn't. But that's no excuse to show fear.** Panic is setting in, which means hurling insults out of reflex as a survival technique. The barbs may be a bit scattered by the sense of worry, and more than a few may be directed at the refs, but you must keep your wits about you and not let the opponent see your fear. Even if you want to piss yourself.

8. **Your team is getting the skin kicked off the kernels of corn in their shit. Time to hide your face.** Welp, you be fucked. Now's when you have to sit and stew in your juices. While getting mocked, lick your wounds and direct all of your white-hot rage at the coaches and players of your own team. Whatever you do, don't get blubbery and emotional. You'll never live it down.

9. **Respect those who have met unintentionally tragic ends.** Otherwise known as the Heath Ledger rule. That means no jokes about Sean Taylor's death, lest you find yourself getting clotheslined and dragged from the back of a pickup truck in the FedEx Field parking lot. On the

other hand, jokes about Ben Roethlisberger's near-fatal motorcycle accident are fair game, because it was danger he brought upon himself by being dumb enough to ride a motorcycle without a helmet. Also, and this is critical, he survived. Not to mention that he's been spotted palling around with Carson Daly. That's more than a venial sin.

10. **Steer clear of extremely derogatory epithets.** If you aren't brave enough to say it when surrounded by a group of said folks, don't say it at all.

11. **Never speak ill of Joey Porter.** THAT'S DISRESPECT! He has ways of knowing, even if you do it in private. And he never forgets. And he will visit any affront to his person tenfold upon your head. With his dogs. He might bite you himself. Scratch that, he will. Fix that mouth good. And then you'll need a rabies shot. They hurt too.

IX.5 "Can You Please Sign My Newborn?": Autograph Hunting

Try not to be alarmed at the news that athletes do not much care for you. In fact, they're plenty freaked out with obsessive fans and have personal security prepared to deal with you. Yes, the glorified idols of sport upon whom you lavish your near-heroin-addiction affection have better things to do than to curry your favor. They have commercials to film for the latest edgy iteration of Gatorade. If it's Peyton Manning, he has a spot to film for every consumer product known to man.

Indeed, NFL players have nothing but disdain to show when you find them in the public sphere. Usually, when this happens at all, it's at one of the many Cheesecake Factories, Best Buys, Olive Gardens, or paintball courses that dot the suburban hinterlands surrounding the city they play in. Because most famous athletes live the secluded lifestyle you would expect of any obscenely wealthy individual, yet have tastes that adhere to your average fifteen-year-old male.

But surely there must be a way to get them to warm up to you and give you a measly signature? Outside of getting bilked at autograph shows, these are your best bets.

Be their server at the Cheesecake Factory. Slip them what appears to be a copy of the bill. After the player foolishly commits his John Hancock to the piece of scrap paper, kindly turn in the uniform you stole from the nineteen-year-old you trussed up outside the restaurant and beam the smile that only comes via the sense of pride from a job well done.

Lay a sob story on them. Because nothing works on a ball of kinetic energy like a good play on the sympathies. Actually, the player will likely cave to your demands to avoid the blubbering you're subjecting them to. Either way, success!

Tell them autographs are part of a video game. There's nothing outside the playing field that athletes respect quite like the gaming world. Get them to think it will advance the cause of their online *Call of Duty* profile and players will sign your week-worn drawers, if need be.

Berate them horribly. As NFL coaches have evinced for decades, football players respond to nothing like infantilizing techniques that rob them of their basic humanity. Now you can turn the denial of their worth to your gain.

Get a hot girl to do it for you. If there's a tactic no NFL player can elude, it's that of the impossibly attractive female decoy. Sure, it's expected, but hot girls tend to get what they want from athletic mental midgets. And book-writing mental midgets, if memory serves.

IX.6 Pester God to Intercede on Your Team's Behalf

Priggish religious types like to chide football fans by saying that praying to God to beseech Him to make their favorite team win is a disgusting perversion of faith. "God has much more important things to deal with," they cry. "He doesn't concern Himself with who wins a measly old football game!" Disregard their sanctimony. Those people are probably all Lions fans who long ago swore allegiance to a dark master in hopes of getting even one win. In fact, no single act works better for increasing your team's chances of victory than groveling to the Man Upstairs. But, mind you, only if it's done properly. God is a stickler for details, because apparently He is in them.

Once you're ready to get started, douse yourself with a bit of holy water. If that's in short supply, beer is a fine substitute. Just make sure it's not a shitty brand, like any of the ones that advertise on NFL broadcasts. Anyway, be sure when praying to face the direction of your team's stadium. Muslim readers may refuse to do this because they are supposed to be facing Mecca, which may explain why NFL teams with a large Muslim fan base do not win very often.

His Godliness gets roughly forty-three million requests from sports fans each day, though half of those are from baseball fans asking Him to cut short their miserable lives. Still, that leaves a very high volume of pleas for intercession on behalf of real sports teams. How He ultimately decides on whom to favor is anyone's guess, though I have an inside source (lots of angels are habitual snitches) who says it boils down to the sheer number of quality pleas he gets from each side. God is very democratic like that. So whenever your team loses a critical game and you didn't get down on your knees and cancel out a rival fan's prayer, you're directly responsible for your team's failure on the field. And you're going to hell. And believe me, it's worse than it sounds because every other demon is a Steelers fan. Which kind of makes it like earth.

At the same time, God doesn't like to be bothered by the same people every single week, so you might want to space out the number of requests throughout the season. Saving them up for a playoff run isn't a bad idea. Above all else, you must exercise restraint. Beg the big guy enough and you're gonna find yourself on the Do Not Bless list.

In a pinch and finding God to be unresponsive to your recent begging, take it up with Satan. He does have a much better return-on-request rate. Unfortunately his price tag is a bit steeper—it's usually your soul, and probably carrying out an evil task like a bridge-bombing of some sort, meaning you can only go to him once every so often (unless you're a fellow collector of souls like Al Davis). So you might want to save him for a Super Bowl or a conference championship game or something else important. You wouldn't believe how many Giants fans' souls he got before Super Bowl XLII. How else do you think they won that game? Sure, Satan loves the Patriots, but he's a guy who puts business first.

IX.7 Fortifying Your Conversations with the Power of Football Clichés

Getting a proper handle on the culture of football requires you to inject a number of phrases Romanowski-like into everyday conversation, as though dropping a mention of the Wildcat Formation into a discussion of health care reform were a perfectly normal thing. Besides supplementing the usual bouquet of expletives, these sayings help pad out your otherwise flabby speech with the added muscular oomph of sport talk. That doesn't mean you need to belabor the terminology of Xs and Os, telling your friends to run slant and go routes to find the bathroom and asking your girl for some better weak-side penetration. Well, maybe give that last one some thought.

Granted, these sayings are entirely devoid of meaning,

but they're a staple of football discourse. Employing them incessantly makes you sound knowing, even when what you actually know about the game could fit on the top of an end-zone pylon. As with everything, it's all about pulling off the act. As a bonus, you'll find these phrases to be very versatile in their usage, applying to situations outside the obvious football context, which only serves to further decrease the time you'll have to spend conversing coherently with others, the bane of any intense gridiron fan.

In some cases, they are familiar toss-off expressions used by players, coaches, and team executives; in others, they're the redundancies and hollow prattle often employed by television announcers. Feel free to borrow liberally from either school of NFL parlance; it will let others know that you are a fan of varied tastes. A pigskin polyglot, if you will.

"At the end of the day . . ."

How It Is Used: A preface to any statement of fact that you feel could benefit from an empty sense of gravity.

It's a useless and meaningless saying, but you won't find a player or coach in the NFL who doesn't toss this one out after every thought in need of verbal underscoring. For example: "Yes, we just lost by five touchdowns at home. We had some plays that didn't go our way, but, at the end of the day, we're still the same fifty-three guys who have to go out there each week."

Use Outside of Football: "Look, I know I drove us to financial ruin, cheated on mom, got her brother arrested and her sister killed, lost the house in a poker game, and sold you kids into slavery, but, *at the end of the day*, we're still a family."

"It is what it is"

How It Is Used: A blanket statement of resignation; an unhelpful way of answering someone asking for specifics.

> *Reporter: "Today you surrendered eight plays of 20 or more yards. The opposition had more than 300 yards rushing by the end of the third quarter. Then their backups scored another three touchdowns on you. How would you describe the play of the defense today?"*
>
> *Athlete: "It is what it is."*

Use Outside of Football:

> *Nosy person: "You're squatting in a closed Domino's Pizza storefront, subsisting on the cheese from discarded pizza boxes, and selling your blood for smokes? Really? Is this what you're planning to do with yourself? You call this living?"*
>
> *You: "It is what it is."*

"Taking it one week at a time"

How It Is Used: A response to any request for speculation in regard to the outcome of future events.

The NFL is an environment in which the entire landscape of the league can change on a week-to-week basis and the slightest boasting gets inflated into bulletin board material. With this in mind, players and coaches don't enjoy engaging in hypothetical discussions. You should do the same.

Use Outside of Football: Overbearing parents inquiring, "When're you getting a job?" Easy: "Lay off, 'rents, I just graduated and *I'm taking life one week at a time*. Who knows what tomorrow will bring." The girlfriend carps: "When are you going to settle down and marry me?" Your winning rejoinder: "You can't live your life that way. When it happens, it happens. *Gotta live your life one week at a time*." Before long, you'll see how far speaking fatalistically can get you and just how easy it is to make Ramen noodles (very easy!). At least Bill Belichick will find you relatable.

"Football move"

How It Is Used: A term with a meaning impossible to pin down, which doesn't stop referees and announcers from using it constantly when detailing a ruling on a fumble, interception, or incomplete pass.

After catching a pass, a receiver or a defender is required to make what is commonly referred to as a "football move" before he is considered to have possession of the ball. If the player loses control of the ball prior to making this "football move," the pass is considered incomplete. However, the exact definition of this term is cryptic at best. Conceivably one could stand in place after catching the ball for an hour, drop it, and have the play considered an incomplete pass. What actions then meet the requirements of a football move? A certain amount of steps taken after the catch? Or is it more a matter of type than degree? Perhaps there's an especially football suggestive motion that a player has to perform? Maybe striking the Heisman pose.

Use Outside of Football: That said, allow uncertainty to work to your advantage when employing this bit of gridiron legalese. If someone calls dibs on something, take it anyway and note that they neglected to make a football move with said item. While they try to make sense of the bullshit you just fed them, you'll have at least a few seconds head start toward the door.

"To throw someone under the bus"

How It Is Used: To malign a teammate's or a coworker's poor performance in public.

In the esprit-de-corps-fueled world of the NFL, loyalty is treasured above all, unless, of course, you're a superstar. Then anything goes. It is therefore considered very bad form to single out a teammate's performance for blame, no matter how glaringly obvious it may be to everyone involved.

Use Outside of Football: Adopt this attitude in your own life. If your wife points out a recent transgression you've committed to another couple, immediately accuse her of throwing you under the bus and undermining the camaraderie of the family. She'll learn her lesson when she sees how much that comment hurts her value on the swinging spousal trading block.

"Trickeration"

How It Is Used: A colloquial way of describing a trick play, which is defined as one that employs laterals, reverses, fake-reverses, the Wildcat formation, flea flickers, harp seals, flaming hoops, a fold-up table for three-card monte, shimmery sound effects, George Lucasonian levels of CGI, and Antwaan Randle El.

It's not so much the actual term trickeration that begs for kidney punches so much as it is the disgusting overuse of the suffix "eration" appended to nouns. Now the act of "cooking," once so froufrou sounding, becomes "cookeration," which is a much more macho if grammatically abortive term. It's like applying barbecue sauce to a carrot stick, seemingly out of place and maybe vaguely disgusting, yet not quite as embarrassing as just eating the carrot stick.

Use Outside of Football: By prostitutes who have yet to master noun endings.

"Sense of urgency"

How It Is Used: A popular idiom often heard in sports broadcast booths to describe when a team is feeling pressure to perform well. Try to puff up your own dialogue with inflated variants of common expressions.

Use Outside of Football: Announcers are never content to say what they mean, not when they have the opportunity to employ high-flown expressions that don't mean anything. It sounds foolish until you try it for yourself. You'll be surprised at how consequential your life suddenly sounds. For instance, instead of saying you don't know where your next month's rent is coming from, say that you feel the sense of impending privation. Doesn't that already sound better?

"If you're . . . , you have to be . . ."

How It Is Used: A way of describing someone in the third person, in which the speaker asks the second person to put themselves in the place of the third person and then tells them what their mental state would be in such a scenario.

Use Outside of Football: No one knows why announcers use this odd construct, but a viewer would be hard-pressed not to hear it at least a half dozen times per game. Instead of saying "Romeo Crennel should be frustrated with the play of his team today," they will say, "If you're Romeo Crennel, you have just got to be utterly devastated with the results out here today." If you find yourself inclined to use the third person in such awkward ways, you probably write legalese for a living.

"Running downhill"

How It Is Used: To describe a ball carrier, most likely a running back, who runs directly toward an opponent's end zone, as opposed to moving backward, laterally toward the sideline, or upward, as if taking an invisible elliptical to the heavens. Essentially the opposite of what Reggie Bush does.

The phrase is, of course, an idiotic misnomer because a football field is mostly flat, save a minor crown for water drainage, hence there are no hills to descend.

Use Outside of Football: Use this phrase if you want

to provoke one of these pedantic taint-sniffers into a fight. Don't worry, they'll be too busy sweating minutiae to dodge your dick punch.

"Overpursue"

How It Is Used: A defender who too aggressively goes after a running back, ignoring the possibility that the ball carrier could cut back and go in another direction, thus burning the defense for a huge gain.

Use Outside of Football: It would make sense to apply this term to someone who pursues a perspective mate with reckless abandon. But then stalkers would lose their preferred verb, and they're not people you want to screw with.

"Impose your will"

How It Is Used: To be able to do what you want despite direct resistance from other parties. An offense will be said to be imposing its will on the defense when it is moving the ball easily even in the face of a well-prepared adversary.

Use Outside of Football: Surely there are a number of occasions in life when one person is able to exert considerable force over another in getting them to do what they want. Lawful occasions, preferably.

"You play to win the game!"

How It Is Used: Nothing less than a mission statement of life; once a mantra used by Herman Edwards to chew out a reporter at a postgame press conference.

Use Outside of Football: In football, as in life, you always want to finish at the top. If you're not winnin', you're dyin'! It's important to remind people of that every once in a while. A belligerent tone and a wild-eyed expression works best.

"It looks like he's just having fun out there"
How It Is Used: A cloying observation in regard to the seemingly whimsical play of quarterback Brett Favre.

Whether it's throwing a pick-six off his back foot or tossing the ball across the field into the welcoming chest of a linebacker playing zone coverage, announcers and analysts are enamored with the play of Brett Favre—so much so that they love to describe his every mannerism on the football field as positively childlike. While some other players have had this remark applied to them by the announcigensia, it is typically reserved for Favre. And it's grating as all hell.

Use Outside of Football: Now, you ask, how can I employ this very specific phrase to my own life? The answer is that you cannot. It is strictly verboten, on penalty of having your balls placed on Rob Bironas's kicking tee. It's the only way you'll learn.

IX.8 Get Tat Up from the Mat Up

Getting tatted up, it's not just for biker gangs, inmates, Marines, and coked-out songstresses anymore. Sports fans have embraced the art of the tattoo in all its eventually regrettable majesty. It's not a stretch to state that the majority of those who suit up on Sundays have some ink on them. But, unlike in the NBA, where old ladies sitting courtside can read off Delonte West's legs as he's throwing the ball in, football players' bodies are better concealed, meaning the only tattoos that fans are usually aware of are the arm tat, the neck tat, and the occasional *Night of the Hunter*–esque knuckle tat. That is, until you catch the player on a blog boozing it up shirtless with two young coeds. You'll be shocked to discover that T-Sizzle looks better in Ole English than you thought.

Among the more well-known tattoos in the NFL are those belonging to Jeremy Shockey (an eagle wrapped in the American flag appears on his right arm), JaMarcus Russell (the words "The Chosen One" are inked on his left arm; presumably "The Underthrowing One" is written on his right), Shawne Merriman (his right forearm bears a light switch in the off position, to signify his "Lights Out" nickname and as a reminder to only inject steroids under the cover of darkness), Kellen Winslow Jr. (a Frederick Douglass quote is inscribed on his left forearm, which no doubt fires up his fellow soldiers), Ray Lewis (has a panther on his right arm, for they prey on witnesses), and Laurence Maroney (has a tattoo of the Kool-Aid guy, which enables him to burst through walls unscathed. If only the same applied to a defense's front seven).

As a fan, there's no reason why you should confine your visual expressions of undying worship to mere trinkets, articles of clothing, and car decals of Calvin pissing on thine enemies. The fan tattoo says a lot of positive things about you, chief among them your commitment and willingness to take pain for your team, both very critical come bar fight time. Believe it or not, the tats serve a pragmatic purpose as well. What would happen if you found yourself waking up naked in the streets without them? Chuckle if you will, but for a football fan, this is hardly a seldom occurrence. How then would freaked-out bystanders know which is your team?

Some may be deterred from getting a fan tattoo for any number of reasons, cop-outs, or bouts of penile inversion. Fear and indecision are the usual excuses. Pay them no mind. Those words are not in the football fan's lexicon. If there's an impulsive and potentially harmful act you could be committing, you're duty-bound to do it.

Supposing it's the day job that poses a problem, it may mean you're in need of a new line of work. Or that you need to dig in your high heels, Nancy. If the boss is thinking there's a conflict between your neck tattoo depicting a buccaneer garroting a saint and your job running a day-care service, let him know that if your rights as a fan are to be impinged upon, you can have a crowd of sixty Bucs fanatics out front within the hour. No way they'll risk it.

On the whole, fan tattoos differ from those of players in several noteworthy ways: they don't scare anybody, and they have a unhealthy store of flab undergirding them. Their purpose is to reflect the team's glory, not to promote the individual's. The athlete, through body art, is trying to tell his own story, and you're turning that story into

Ron Howard–like hagiography. The athlete tats also have more room for idiosyncrasies, as with LaMarr Woodley's large Woody Woodpecker image on his left bicep, while the menu of fan options is narrower, but not without character. For example, if you got a Woody tattoo, that bird better have the team's helmet on it and it better be pecking the shit out some treelike representation of your rival.

Collage of Greats—Ever dreamt of being a living, breathing, pantheon of greatness for your franchise? Now's your chance. Lionize the great players and the achievements of the team with stoic-looking portraits of players coupled with title banners, Lombardi trophies, whatever. The crux here is that you're forced to plan for the future. While acknowledging the titans and titles of the past (if applicable), you must leave real estate vacant for future Super Bowl insignias. If you leave too little space, are you selling your team short? If you leave too much, are you setting yourself up for disappointment? If you're a Browns fan, you're liberated from this worry.

Boring Old Team Logo—Clear the way, everybody—here comes Thrilly McPushingtheenvelope! Way to be daring. Yeah, everybody loves to prostrate themselves before the graven idol of team imagery, but true fandom behooves at least a semblance of effort.

Caricaturized Scary Version of Team Mascot—That's a little more like it. Have that big intimidating cardinal on your back looking all jacked up and blow-

ing alarming amounts of smoke out of its beak. Given
a deft artistic touch, even the most seemingly benign
team mascot has the potential to rattle. Doubtful of
the potential of the 49ers' grizzled old prospector to
look imposing? Careful, he can swing that pickax
awful hard! Or blind you with his daily ration of flour!

Autograph Tattoos—One newish trend in fan
tattoos involves getting an autograph from a player,
taking that 'graph to a tattoo artist, and having a
replica of that signature writ large on your body. It's
almost as if the player branded you like livestock.
Which is actually kind of a good look if you're one of
the Hogettes.

Copying Players' Tats—As the axiom goes, imita-
tion is the sincerest form of flattery. It's also the first
warning sign of stalking. Even more worrisome is the
tendency to allow the blinding passion of fandom to
obscure the discerning eye of good taste (already not a
strong suit among football fans).

The Date Your Team Was Founded—Usually
reserved for the followers of longstanding franchises,
such as the Bears, Packers, Giants, Steelers, Browns,
Lions, or Redskins, fans of more contemporary
teams can tout that they've been around since the
very beginning. For the Texans fan, that means cel-
ebrating the year of both the founding of their team
and the creation of Friendster. Fitting, considering
they've both been rendered irrelevant in but a few
short years.

Area Code Tattoo—An en vogue method of showing hometown pride and a way of proving to the haters that your community has phone service. The problem is, unless you live in one of the three or four most populous cities, no one has a clue what part of the country it stands for. For example, Darren McFadden has the number 501 tattooed on his right bicep, which most believe is the area code assigned to a pair of his Levi's. So when he says he's got hoes in that area code, he ain't kidding.

Some Supposedly Cool-looking Foreign Bullshit—When all else fails, pick out something flashy and exotic. Dumb people love garish shit that makes no sense, which explains the continued career of McG. Scores of athletes have Maori tattoos they don't understand. Dolphins defensive end Matt Roth, not to take a challenge lying down, takes cultural misappropriation to a new level. Roth has the Chinese characters tattooed 疼闹扑权 on his right arm, which he claims means his last name, but actually translates to "a painful noise rushes at authority."

ARTICLE X

Death: Because Only Al Davis Can Live Forever

X.1 Retirement, or "Which Team Do I Like, Again?"

Glorioski! Prolonging insanity long enough to reach retirement is no gimme achievement. Familial and workplace stressors work in tandem to grind every last shred of life force out of the tired bodylike husk you become by your fifties. To make it this far, you must have found your niche in the world, maybe even landed your dream job, unless that was playing in the NFL, in which case you almost certainly expired before the age of sixty-five.

Now that you've made it to your golden years, whiling away the remainder of your days focusing on what truly matters becomes a heavenly reality. One that is tempered by the rapid loss on your mental faculties. Surely by now that team has managed to secure at least one title for you. If so, a good chunk of your life has been spent basking in those glorious moments. With your mind swiftly deteriorating, you can safely block out the bad, while keeping the broken record of highlights from the good times rolling. Perhaps even embellishing them a tad. You were, after all, having a threesome with two Japanese gravure idols when David Tyree made his helmet catch, right?

Time passes more quickly when you have little idea what is going on. That's why Joe Gibbs's second stint with the Redskins felt to him like a half hour. That's detrimental for maintaining a normal social life, but that was never really a priority for you anyway. This way, though, off-seasons will pass like commercial breaks. March will melt into August like so much cheese on Taco Bell's latest fully loaded heart-attack special. Before you know it, the regular season has rolled around again.

Better yet, free time and disposable income means complete devotion can be paid to your favorite team during the season. While other suckers, smug with full control of their bowels, must squander time carrying out a fully rounded life, you're free to be as single-minded as you wish. What better way do you have to spend your time? Crocheting bath mats? Rewriting your will? Detaching and reattaching your colostomy bag? Surely you can do better.

For starters, securing a routine for the season needs to move to the top of your bucket list, right after punching anyone who has actually compiled a bucket list. Your kids are grown, your responsibilities are gone. If you haven't made your way through the waiting list for season tickets by the time you've reached dotage, you've erred in life. Did you buy a boat? Bother to send your kids to college?

If those freeloaders can't ball well enough to get a scholarship, you'd best cast them by the wayside before they become a further drain on your resources.

Tune the family out. Finesse that senility with signs of lucidity, or chances are you'll be stuck in a home. Bear in mind that retirement homes, in addition to being brutal houses of death, don't have NFL Sunday Ticket, much less liquor outside the administrator's office. Any football discussion will be limited to nurses using football metaphors to get you to swallow pills. Do show at least enough coherence to remember family members' names, maybe even a birthday or two. Try to combine your interests by letting them know you're aware of which team they like, preferably by insulting that team. If you've succeeded in making them all follow the same team as you, demonstrate your cognizance by occasionally saying something derogatory about a rival team. If that comment is met with an attempt to make a high five, do your best to make contact. They won't expect more than a timid effort on your part, so at least give them that much.

Failing that, at least keep your jersey on at all times. Your family can't possibly put someone away with his game face on.

X.2 Your Team Relocated to Another City! Your Entire Life Was All For Naught!

Fans maintain a love-hate relationship with their team's ownership—in turns irritated by personnel moves and escalating ticket, parking, and concession prices—but in the end they somehow remain fiercely loyal to the miserly, unfeeling tycoon running the show. Love is an easily exploitable emotion like that.

But what happens when an owner pulls the rug out from under their fans by moving the team to another city? As those wronged by Robert Irsay, Art Modell, and Bud Adams can attest, a violent sense of betrayal capped by a bloodlust worthy of Patrick Bateman. And why not? This is the destruction of people's livelihoods on a massive scale, usually for no other reason than a city not relenting on the owner's demands for unnecessary new digs filled with luxury suites and cushy escape pods in the untimely event of a proletariat uprising.

Though franchises in large markets such as New York, Chicago, and Philadelphia are immune to this sort of exodus, it seems every other year at least one team is rumored to be on the move. Whenever this happens, Los Angeles is usually at or near the top of the list of likely destinations, in spite of the overwhelming evidence that L.A. is a horrible pro football town. Sure, L.A. has some great college and high school teams, but it also has a track record of two failed NFL franchises, coupled with no reason to believe one would work there now. Los Angeles remains a glorious mirage to the football owner, perhaps because of the City of Angels' large population, its prestige, or its fans' habits of showing up right before halftime and leaving midway through the fourth quarter. It's the ever-present holy grail for the disgruntled owner in search of new revenue, whereas somehow Las Vegas, one of the largest growing markets in the country, with its wondrous legalized gambling, merits only the occasional murmur.

A strange quirk of fandom is that it is inextricably linked to the city where the team is based. If a team skips town, it doesn't take its fans with it, no matter how die-hard. In the era of free agency, where player turnover can overhaul a roster within the span of a few years, a team's location is the only constant. Even if you didn't grow up in the town where your team is based, so much of that team's identity is anchored in that city. An essential component of trash-talk among fans is bashing the city a team calls home. Through years of defending the team in these verbal battles, you've learned to embrace the character of that town as a means of backing the team.

So when the team moves, it loses the soul that under-pins it, even if it keeps the same name and uniforms. Can anyone honestly say the Indianapolis Colts evoke the same set of images that the Baltimore Colts do? Of course not. The only way the modern Colts could seem whiter is if they played in Utah.

Protect your precious history. Petition the league to negate all the history from the relocated franchise prior to departing. The organization's title tally should go back to zero. Any Hall of Famers belong to the old hometown. Art Modell, scumbag though he is, left the team Cleveland Browns' history and name in Cleveland when leaving after the 1995 season. The Colts and Titans weren't kind enough to do the same for Baltimore and Houston when they skipped town. Considering the history of the Oilers up to that point, it may have been for the best.

Abandon fandom altogether. This is an understandable, if harrowing option. The pain of losing a team can open your eyes to the ruthless business-driven underbelly of the league, and you just won't be able to look at football the same way again. The remainder of your days can be spent constructively plotting the "accidental" death of the owner who jilted your town. If I could recommend a method, I think sarin gas is woefully underutilized in matters of petty vengeance, but that's just me.

Adopt your former rivals. After the Browns left Cleveland for Baltimore following the 1995 season, many Browns fans jumped ship to join the Steelers' fan base, if only for a few years. Judge them harshly if you will. It seems like heresy until you're put in that position. Some folks just can't go on without football, and while taking on the torch of a team that is merely good smacks of bandwagon jumping, the rival is at least a familiar figure. After all, the closest emotion to hatred is love. And everyone loves a good hate fuck.

Stick with the franchise. Ah, the sports version of Stockholm syndrome, where victimized fans dutifully stick with the franchise even after being played for saps. These weak-kneed individuals have been cuckolded by another city, yet pine for their former team from afar. It's as though your wife runs off with another man and you respond by spending your days masturbating to her image. C'mon, dude, have some self-respect.

What, then, are we to make of fans who reap the benefits of a relocated team? What amount of culpability do they share for pulling for an ill-gotten franchise? Have they no empathy? To aid and abet a moneygrubbing owner, they become accomplices in the high crime of team larceny. And what of the case of Ravens fans, who bitched endlessly about having the Colts leave town in the middle of the night in 1984 only to accept another team with open arms after it screwed over another city? What good is it to sacrifice your soul if all you get in return is the Ravens?

X.3 Buying a Team Means Buying the Affections of Millions, Even as You Screw Them

Holy shit, you've struck it rich! How did you amass this fortune? Was it through grit, determination, hard work, and savvy decision-making? Fuck that. That's for chumps. Most likely it was through questionable business practices and outright white-collar criminal behavior. Or maybe you just inherited it all. That's how it's done in this country.

But that's not really important. What matters is if it's enough to purchase an NFL team. To even have a shot at that holy grail, you'll be needing some serious fuck-you money. Enough to make the average CEO cry the tears of the most down-and-out pauper. Enough to have your face chiseled on the big Jesus statue in Rio de Janeiro. Basically, what Oprah's got.

This is not an easy gravy train to board. In 2008, for the first time, the value of the average NFL franchise topped $1 billion, and it's only going up, even in tough economic times. That's even factoring in the thirteen thousand dollars the Texans are worth. Team ownership is a massive investment, but one that will pay mega dividends in the not too distant future. Indeed, once in the owner's box, you'll be fleecing your fans and local taxpayers in no time at all. Just make sure you get a controlling interest of the franchise. An owner with minority interest in a team is in no better position than your average Packer fan, as that franchise has been a publicly traded, nonprofit corporation since 1923. The day you find yourself no better than a Packer fan is the day you take a romantic bath with a plugged-in hairdryer. If you're not going to be the one calling the shots, what's the point? Sharing in the massive profits is all well and good, but it's nothing more than obscene riches without the clout to back it up.

Billionaires don't have as many lifestyle choices as conventional wisdom would lead you to believe. Social pressures exist for them too. As people who've committed their whole life to superficial pleasures, they feel it more keenly than most. They must follow in lockstep the few paths considered acceptable to someone of their outsize means, and they are as follows: owning a sports team, running for political office, or getting into philanthropy.

The first is for homespun narcissists. The second is for deluded self-righteous assholes. The last is for noble idiots. It should come as no surprise that George W. Bush is a few donations from pulling off the trifecta.

The downside to the process of bidding for a team is that it's not merely a function of having the money, but also of having the connections that will get you considered as a candidate for ownership. First, there obviously has to be a team up for sale or an expansion franchise being proposed. And don't think there aren't handfuls of billionaires waiting in the wings to snatch the golden egg out from under you.

Like any collection of influential rich people, the old boys and girls club that constitutes NFL ownership likes to vet perspective buyers before they join the inner circle. They want to see if the business ties you have will reflect well on the league. They also need to make sure you've carried out the requisite slew of contract kills that forms initiation. They want to know that you're one of them, that you're not some Mark Cuban–esque gadfly who will challenge league orthodoxy and make fellow owners look out of touch. Most of all, they want to know that you're not a minority.

So what kind of owner will you be? A benevolent champion of the fan who keeps in mind the true spirit of the league? One who doesn't emphasize making money first and offers former players generous post-career benefits? Well, you'd be the first. Except you'd never get awarded ownership rights in the first place, so leave those magnanimous leanings at the door. Those interested in joining this elite club must conform to one of the following personality types.

IMPERIOUS NAPOLEONIC MEGALOMANIAC

The NFL loves to exercise complete, almost suffocating control over how the media covers the league. Why else would it ban even mainstream media Web sites from posting footage of league action longer than thirty seconds? That's why any owner who wants to buy up every media property in his market and punish the ones who cover his team unfavorably is ready to belong to this politburo.

Example: Dan Snyder

OVERWEENING DISRUPTIVE CARTOONISH MEGALOMANIAC

Every ownership group needs a brash character who thinks he's a bigger star than the players he puts on the field. Hoping to win at any cost, this owner will offer a refuge to the most troubled athlete. Volatile situations are never in short supply when he welcomes the most uncoachable superstars and pairs them with meek, unassertive head coaches.

Example: Jerry Jones

Decrepit Delusional Megalomaniac

The most dysfunctional of the megalomaniacal subset, those representing this type were usually once savvy and hard-charging renegades who fell victim to old age and their overpowering sense of paranoia. They do make for good press-conference footage, though.

Example: Al Davis

Aristocratic Collaborator with the Russians

These guys? Oh, they're great. Run a tight ship, they do. They always seem to bring on the right personnel, like the ex-KGB guys whom they lavish with Super Bowl rings. Just like the one watching me type this right now. He sure glares at you with bone-chilling seriousness.

Example: Bob Kraft

Leading Republican Donor

What good is a bunch of rich old white people if they're not funneling money to the GOP? Wouldn't want the NFL to be branded a terrorist organization, now, would we? Especially with all those bombs flying around the field of play.

Examples: Alex Spanos, Woody Johnson

Upstanding Boring Old Guy

The ownership group can always use some fusty old guys who know the league from its heyday. The difficulty here for newcomers is that these people come from families that have long been involved with the league. And most former players typically succumb to painful conditions sustained during their career before they have time to cobble the money together. At least they have thirty-eight-member pregame announcing teams to join.

Examples: Dan Rooney, Jerry Richardson

Penny-Pinching Cancerous Fuckwit

If they had their druthers, these owners would just as soon pay the parking attendants to suit up on gameday than pour any money into the product on the field. They alienate their fans, yet take years to fire patently incompetent employees. A study of poor management, they test the limits of fan patience. And if they show their faces in public, the limits of a fan's brick-throwing arm.

Examples: Mike Brown, Bill Bidwill, William Clay Ford, Sr.

Megatycoon Who Owns Multiple Sports Teams

The only thing that owners respect more than money is a shitload of money. Just so long as they keep their NBA and Premier League teams far, far away from our football.

Example: Paul Allen, Malcolm Glazer

Mr. Home Depot Man

Because the NFL could use the founders of more companies with atrocious customer service. Is the founder of Best Buy interested in purchasing a team? He'd fit right in.

Example: Arthur Blank

THE GUYS WHO DON'T MUCH LIKE WHERE THEIR TEAM IS LOCATED

No one said you have to love the market you inherit. This is a business, after all. Why should you look with anything other than contempt at the people who have supported your business over the years? It's not like they're your immediate family.

Examples: Ralph Wilson, Tom Benson, Zygi Wilf

RELATIVES OF PREVIOUS OWNERS

Yeah, remember when I said this was a tough crowd to break into? Wasn't lying. Swearing and blaspheming, yes, but not lying. Sports franchises tend to stay family possessions for a good long while, meaning your best hope was probably to have married into one of these clans. Instead you choose to spend your life becoming a self-made success. That's okay. Half the owners in the league didn't grow up rooting for the team they own now. Do you really want to associate with people like that?

Examples: Clark Hunt, Jim Irsay, John Mara, Steve Tisch, Denise York, Virginia McCaskey, Mike Brown, Dan Rooney, Chip Rosenbloom

X.4 Remain Die-hard Even When You're About to Die

It's a tragic eventuality that our bodies will suffer the ravages of age, leaving us as immobile and useless as Drew Bledsoe, at least until a special kind of water pill is developed that will keep us from growing old. Bill Parcells is hard at work screaming at scientists for this to happen.

For the time being, we must brave the murky fog of senility to root on for our favorite team, even if it means pissing ourselves slightly more often than in our younger days. We may not be able to throw back the booze like we used to, may not be able to toss the ball around at the tailgate anymore, and may not have gotten it up in a decade, but our passion for the game is no less strong.

How does one conquer the limitations placed upon us by bodily rot? A strict regiment of drugs, mostly. Other than that, you've got to remember to go easy on yourself. Conserving your strength is a must. Don't waste energy fighting with the staff stealing your money at the nursing home when there are senior fans of other teams to scrap with.

The culture of football is a distinctly Darwinian one. No quarter is shown to the elderly fan, nor should he expect any. There will be many instances when, pulling for his favorite team, the fan of advanced age will be confronted with the threats of a younger, more able-bodied rival, who, in addition to superior coordination and strength, touts the full use of his bladder and extremities.

On paper, this looks like a mismatch. But it needn't be an immediate cause for alarm. Indeed, the cliché that old age and treachery will always overcome the forces of youth and Dutch courage is true, especially in instances where the old guy isn't cornered and able to bribe the kid to leave him in peace.

Generally, though, the young are malleable and can be dealt with using a few simple tricks that are also effective on household pets. It's important to get them down pat, since more young miscreants will be on the streets with the Democrats controlling the White House again.

The key is to be well-armed. Who's gonna suspect the elderly? Not the cocky young asshole who thinks himself invincible, that's for sure. Of course, this strategy is best suited for altercations outside the stadium. Inside, past searches at the gate, you'll have to hang close to ushers and medical staff.

X.5 To a Bears Fan Dying Young

Today we gather to celebrate the life of Kevin Murawski, father, patriot, amateur pornography enthusiast, pipe fitter, closet sestina writer, and most of all, Bears fan. One hell of a Bears fan at that.

If ever there was a true Monsters of the Midway fan, it was Kevin. His mark of 461 consecutive games watched is a Herculean feat that few can say they have equaled. Even when his health declined, he made sure there was nothing that got between him and his beloved team. We all remember the game against Detroit where he showed up at Soldier Field with the colostomy pouch in tow. I bet that guy in the Herman Moore jersey regrets ever talking trash to him while he was in throwing range.

Kevin loved his team and all the tradition that surrounded it. It was always a great source of pride for him that the NFC championship trophy was named after George Halas. Any year the Bears didn't go to the Bowl, he'd remark during the trophy presentation, "That's our trophy. We're just lettin' 'em borrow it for a year." A douchey sentiment? Surely. More grating every time he did it? Absolutely. But it brought him joy during an otherwise dour moment. And he was good for that. When others thought the worst of the Bears, he played the optimist, even beyond the bounds of reason. He defended each of the pitiful quarterbacks who has come through the Bears organization in the past twenty years, logic be damned.

Rick Mirer? "Shows incredible poise, even when forcing wounded ducks into double coverage."

Craig Krenzel? "He was very clutch in college at Ohio State. That's bound to surface in the pros if we give him a few more seasons under center."

Kordell Stewart? "Any quarterback fast enough to chase down the defensive backs who catch his passes is a real asset."

Moses Moreno? "He might not be any good, but starting a Hispanic quarterback sends a positive message about the franchise being open to inept quarterbacks of all colors."

Not Rex Grossman, however. There were limits even to Kevin's blind homerism.

Let there be no doubt that his was a full life. Kevin's father made a point of telling him he was conceived the evening the Bears won the NFL championship in 1941, which is still an uncomfortable fact even in death. Had he not had a bad case of whiskey dick, he might have accomplished the same feat when Chicago won Super Bowl XX. Indeed, witnessing the '85 Bears' prolific run was one of the great thrills of life, a fact he made sure to remind people of on a near hourly basis. Like many fans, he begrudged Mike Ditka for not allowing an aged Walter Payton to get a score in the historic reaming of the Patriots. A copy of the tearful apology letter we wrote to Sweetness the week after the game remains framed on his living room wall.

The Bears meant everything to him, which made it really easy for him to blot out the important emotional connections he made over the years. His wife Diane was his loving, and loved, companion, as fiercely loyal to him as he was to his football team. As many of you know, when she first met Kevin, she was a Packers fan. Only through kind jostling and a series of maybe-kidding-but-maybe-not threats did he bring her around to the Bears' side. Her capacity for love was enough to overlook this bit of fan manipulation, or at least so we all thought until she turned their children into followers of the Pack. He still found it in his heart to give them his undying love, at least for thirty weeks out of the year.

We can take comfort knowing he's gone to a better place—one where Dick Jauron is not—at least until pitchfork-wielding Buffalo fans dismember him. We shouldn't think of his passing as an extinguishing of the torch of fandom, but as an opening of another choice seat at the stadium. I know most of you are awaiting the reading of his will, but as soon as the executor of his estate can make sense of it through all the greasy brat stains, we'll be sure to report who gets what.

Let us pour out some Old Style and sing a round of "Bear Down, Chicago Bears" for our fallen comrade. It's what he would want as a dying wish. That and Lambeau Field being carpet bombed into the Stone Age, but we're still cobbling together the funds for that one. In the meantime, let's pull a Cedric Benson and get shitfaced and make some bad decisions.

X.6 Hector Your Favorite Players into the Hall of Fame

Upon reaching an advanced age, you want to be comforted in the knowledge that your life signified a lasting, greater Something. For most, it's a struggle to define what that legacy was. Absent an easy revelation, the average person will fall back on heavy doses of delusion, empty accolades, and a collection of grubby snot-nosed grandchildren. But if your life was comprised mainly of yelling slander about people's moms in support of a football team, seeing the players you valued most immortalized in the Hall of Fame becomes life's remaining goal. Even if that recognition comes in the form of an ugly, urine-colored jacket and a bust that looks nothing at all like the cherished athlete it honors.

That validation of the premier players of your era being inducted into the Hall of Fame takes on the utmost importance, not only because those players were critical fixtures for your team over an extended period of time, but because they prove to future generations that your salad days of fandom were of merit. And that they missed something special. Redskins fans shamelessly lobbied for a decade to get famously boring wide receiver Art Monk in the Hall, to the point that that's all they talked about on sports radio shows, during dinner, in the middle of sex, or even to the dutiful postal carriers desperately looking for an out. They harangued anyone who would listen for so long that Monk was finally allowed into Canton, most likely just to appease these singularly obsessed buttholes. And, you know, once he and Darrell Green got in the same year, the 'Skins fans quieted down some. Just goes to show that being unbearable has its benefits sometimes.

Some players are obvious shoo-ins to be inducted into the Hall of Fame. For those world-beaters, there's little fans have to do to ply their case to the forty-four-member Pro Football Hall of Fame Board of Selectors. It's the stars with less than megawattage, those having a résumé with stats in the upper tier but not at the top, and those not fortunate enough to be a member of a dynasty who will challenge fans to put together a compelling case. The board you have to convince is a fastidious lot, accustomed as they are to being sucked up to by fans and being dismissed out of hand by players. Just the recipe for twisting any otherwise normal individual into a sad, embittered, crotchety husk of a douche.

Bribing the selection committee that is responsible for enshrining candidates into the Hall is no easy task. Any finalist for induction must receive at least 80 percent of the vote from paunchy white guys who never played the sport. So it's going to take more than simply prevailing upon them to acknowledge that the player in question is great. Get to know them, know their vices, know their biases. Thirty-two of them are media representatives from cities where a team is located (New York has two). If there's anyone who can be bought off with cheap shit, it's members of the mainstream media. For the majority of them, it doesn't take anything more than a six-inch Subway sandwich. The less healthy the better. Nothing butters up sports writers like sugar cookies slathered in cake batter.

Of the remainders, eleven are at-large members and one is a member of the Pro Football Writers of America. The at-large guys are national NFL writers who are no less susceptible to the spoils of gift baskets and topless photos of Peyton Manning. What makes them most difficult to convince is that they are wont to retain petty grudges against any player you like, whether or not the incident that sparked the grudge occurred within the last fifteen years. Most likely, said incident happened when the player was a rookie and had to blow off the writer for an entirely justifiable reason. Being a sad, cantankerous old turdlet, the writer has held onto this enmity for long enough to get his kids in on the act. Hate to break it to you, but there's nothing a fan can do to reverse the grudge. Once writers have antipathy set in their minds for the tiniest slight by a player, they'll never let it go. You might as well put their induction out of your mind. Unless you get compromising photos of said writer after-hours in flagrante at the aquarium. Len Pasquarelli knows what I mean. If you can pull that, make your reservations for summer in Canton soon, while you can still only be minorly fleeced by the packages.

X.7 On Death and Deep-frying

Like every storied NFL career, every life eventually comes to a close, though not without considerable kicking and screaming and pitiful attempts to hang on as long as possible, possibly in the form of a comeback with the Jets. Incidentally, that sentence marked the only time in your life the phrase "storied NFL career" has been applied to you. Quite a thrill, I bet. It's nice to have that happen before you check out.

There are a number of things you can do to ready yourself for your passing. The first matter to consider is clearing up the division of your estate. The house, the stock options, the priceless collection of signed throwback jerseys, drawer after drawer full of enchanted undergarments for big games.

Passing off season tickets to a next of kin is the most significant of these considerations. For some, this decision is made easy by circumstance. Maybe you have no kids or only one. Or only one that you choose to acknowledge.

Those who condemned themselves to an early grave with multiple offspring are forced to choose between the squabbling hellions. Which one of them demonstrated more zeal for the team? Which one accompanied you to games with the express purpose of driving your drunk ass home? Which had the fastest response time to your requests for beer? Which is actually willing to pay the excessive personal seat license fees?

Don't be afraid to let your kids know in your waning years that they are in direct competition with each other for the prize. It ensures a considerable delay in the inevitable placement in a retirement home, let alone fewer smarmy remarks when you let one loose in your pants. It's also really fun to watch. Fight! Fight for my love!

As for dying itself, I can't promise you it's going to be pleasant. In fact, it's probably going to be agonizing, not unlike the feeling of having a harpoon jammed into your peehole, only spread over your entire body. Well, man up. Going over the middle for a tough catch ain't no Swiss picnic either, and that only stops pussies like Todd Pinkston from doing it.

On the other hand, it could be relatively benign. Who knows for sure? Definitive research is somewhat lacking on the subject. Another reason to chide non-sports-fans for the failures of science.

What you can know beforehand is that it is your duty to represent your team even in passing. Unless you were found to have switched teams at some point in your life, in which case your corpse will be swaddled in cat-urine-soaked blankets and tossed from a Jeep into the most jackal-filled clearing that can be found. Once they've picked the carcass clean, the clearing will be bombed.

For the honorable fan, splurging on ridiculously expensive NFL licensed merchandise one last time is a fitting send-off. Take the real life example of James Henry Smith, a fifty-five-year-old Pennsylvania man who passed away in 2005. For the viewing, Smith's family had the funeral home place his body in a recliner facing a television playing Steelers highlights, remote control in hand. Truly this is an exemplar of a loving and obedient family. Don't expect much the same out of yours unless you provide them with detailed instructions laying out exactly how to give you the last good-bye.

Be specific to the letter in expressing your final wishes. Spell out in breathtaking detail your vision of having your urn placed in the front seat of a car packed with C-4 and driven into a Patriots fans tailgate (having a Massachusetts license plate that reads FUPATS adds a special flourish to your final blaze of glory). Cremation not your thing? Instruct family members to befriend grounds crew members at the stadium. Getting buried under the fifty-yard line will give you a privileged resting place that only a select circle of fans and Jimmy Hoffa have enjoyed.

I'll implore you to be so anal as to list which highlights you would like to be played during this tribute. Nice catches that come in games the team lost are too bittersweet for eternal repose. Also note that several companies offer urns and caskets emblazoned with team logos. Don't let those maggots chewing on your body after you're buried be confused about where your allegiances lie.

If at all possible, die in a public place. You'll probably get hauled off in an ambulance. Done properly, it will have the appearance of an NFL player being carted off the field. If you can ward off the reaper long enough to make it to the hospital, you can give the onlooking gawkers the famed thumbs up from the stretcher. Finally, in death, you're living the fantasy.

X.8 The Afterlife, or As It's Known in Football-Speak, the Post-Life

See? Death wasn't so bad. The excruciating pain lasted, at most, mere days. You got off easy. A Browns fan has a similar sensation stretched over an entire lifetime. The bright side: no matter how you acted in life, you can spend eternity watching the NFL. Even hell isn't so cruel as to deny you that, as Satan needs the gambling revenue. The rub is that you're forced to watch the games with Eagles fans and only get the broadcasts with Phil Simms doing commentary.

If you satisfy the stringent requirements needed to get into heaven, well, you're likely insufferably boring. But also in luck, for heaven is a fan's paradise in addition to being a regular paradise. Massive HD flat screens everywhere, no hangovers, unlimited tap beer, top shelf whiskey and wings, and, best of all, no Cowboys fans.

Without responsibilities and with an eternity of free time laid out before you, there's no pressure not to act like a meddling asswipe all the time. Feel free to arbitrarily manipulate the fortunes of teams, individuals, or millions of fantasy leagues. Watch the Chargers' cheerleaders gnaw away at their edible uniforms after the game (because you know that's what happens). What in this mortal coil would be a drain on your time or would land you in hot water becomes a perfectly devious undertaking in the afterlife. You've got nothing but time to undermine the course of natural events.

Now's your chance to finally influence the games you love so dear. Haunting players on rival teams is not only a pleasure but incredibly effective. Peyton Manning's early career playoff implosions were the direct result of the enterprising spirit of one bitterly departed Baltimore Colts fan. NFL players are haunted all the time. It's one of the unspoken drawbacks of the game. The haunting is actually the cause of a lot of the drug use in the league. When you're already seeing stuff that weird, you might as well, right? Once you build up some clout up there, they'll even let you deflect the occasional field goal. Scott Norwood isn't going to be pleasant when he meets the ghost who caused that one.

Even off-seasons become less unbearable, as the all-time greats stage daily games spread across a host of heavenly stadia. They can't stop doing it, because Gene Upshaw negotiated a bad deal with the angels running the show. As in life, the afterlife grants favors to the athletically inclined. That's why there are far more former Raiders in heaven than you would have ever thought possible. Pressing questions about who is the best ever are answered on a daily basis. If only sportswriters weren't consigned to the most chemical fiery circle of hell, they'd be awfully depressed, what with the absence of space for pointless speculation . . .

Because in heaven you get to pick how you would like to appear to others for eternity, all the players are in their athletic prime and there's a blissful abundance of hot cheerleaders. The one drawback: your grandparents and great grandparents are also young-looking and screwing all the time. It's gross.

EPILOGUE

This Book Gets Summ-ed Up!
Clap, Clap, Clap-Clap-Clap!

The cliché goes that men lead lives of quiet desperation. Had Thoreau lived to witness the NFL, he'd have seen that fans found a better way of being, a path of loud, intoxicated, worshipful desperation. Given the quality of his playoff beard, he probably would have liked it.

A self-serious person will often try to tell the fan that he squanders the gift of life. That he is crazed because his emotions swing wildly based on the outcome of trivial events that were never in his control. That he is belligerent to his peers, neglectful of his family, and slovenly in appearance.

The fan usually responds by calling him a bitch.

In spite of crass behavior, fans give purpose to great events. We create the possibility for human achievement, because the great among us require the approbation of others. We also need a pack of people to jump into after a touchdown.

People in all walks of life are fans of something, whether it is the arts, politics, science, or tentacle porn. and we all look ridiculous when caught up with the object of our adoration. The only difference is that football fans made the right pick in what to follow. Sure, we are not always shown the loyalty we give. Fans exhibit fiery passion for a team that bilks them and generally takes their love for granted. but still we cheer, hoping for those transcendent moments when we are reminded why we show up each week. And, failing that, holding a good buzz.

Rewards come in the form of wins, championships, and the occasional sloppy parking-lot blow job. These are great moments, memories to last a lifetime. Oddly enough, it's not necessarily what keeps us coming back. Those revelations come when we discover that the rest of life is a procession of deadening tedium between chances to tie one on. And if you can do it while getting crazy over some football, all the better.